D0114623

that's amore

that's

A SON REMEMBERS
DEAN MARTIN

amore

RICCI MARTIN
with Christopher Smith

Taylor Trade Publishing
Lanham • New York • Oxford

Published by Taylor Trade Publishing
A Imprint of the Rowman & Littlefield Publishing Group
4720 Boston Way
Lanham, Maryland 20706

Distributed by National Book Network

Designed by David Timmons

Library of Congress Cataloging-in-Publication Data

Martin Ricci
That's amore : a son remembers Dean Martin / Ricci Martin with Christopher Smith
p. cm.
Includes index.
ISBN 0-87833-272-3 (cloth)
1. Martin, Dean, 1917-1995 . 2. Entertainers—United States—Biography. 3. Martin, Ricci. I. Smith, Christopher, 1961- . II. Title.
PN2287 .M52 M29 2001
791'.092—dc21
[B] 2001037526

∞™ The paper used in this publication meets the minimum requirements of American National Standard for Information Sciences—Permanence of Paper for Printed Library Materials, ANSI/NISO Z39.48-1992.
Manufactured in the United States of America.

Frontispiece: Dean and Ricci, 1955.
Page vi: Dean, Jeanne, and Ricci Martin, November 18, 1953.

Contents

Introduction

I suppose this book started around our family dinner table decades ago. My mom always had one rule—besides the one about no hand grenades in the house—and that was no matter what events were transpiring in our individual worlds, we all were expected to be seated at the dinner table at 6 P.M. nightly for the family meal. It was there, in the cacophony of relaying the important developments of the day, requests to "please pass the mashed potatoes," and the usual banter that comes with seven kids, two parents, and assorted grandparents gathered around one table, that so many stories and memories found a place to take root.

Later, that dinner table conversation would be transported from the family home to restaurants, dark little Italian cafés in Beverly Hills with names like La Famiglia or La Dolce Vita, or a table at the Hamburger Hamlet, the air aged with the smell of grilled onions and cigarette smoke. These were places where the race car of life seemed to take a pit stop, yielding a moment to reflect and reminisce before roaring off into the next curve. At the end of the race, you realize how short those moments really were.

Maybe, then, this book is an attempt to capture some of those stories before they are lost to time. This is what I remember from childhood, my teenage years, and then adulthood as the son of Dean Martin, the entertainer. It's a personal version of family history, either witnessed firsthand or recalled from things

I was told by parents, siblings, relatives, and friends. It may not completely shatter any of the myths, but it will challenge a few of the tired clichés.

Being the son of Dean Martin brings with it certain expectations that were forged from Dad's public image. For instance, whenever I mix my own version of one of Dad's favorite "orangey" drinks—his term for a vodka and orange juice screwdriver—there seems to be an undue amount of attention paid to the paleness of the cocktail. Such is the Dean Martin legacy, even if it's a bit overwrought.

As with most sons and daughters, there comes a perceived duty to stand up for good old Dad, no matter how much he might protest that he certainly didn't need his children defending his honor. In 1992, when *Time* magazine wrote a review of a biography about Dad that drew some unsavory and—I felt—overly broad conclusions about the kind of person he was, I fired off a letter trying to set the record straight. Dad's response was, "Thanks, pallie, but why'd you do that?" After a half-century of living life in the crosshairs of public scrutiny, he had developed a much thicker skin for the occasional poke than had those of us closest to him.

At times, he was noncombative to a fault. Few things really made him mad. I doubt that even the way he was characterized in some of the obituaries published after his death on Christmas Day 1995 at age 78—"boozy," "slacker," "Hollywood lightweight," "womanizer," "never gave a rat's pack about anything"—would have generated more than a brush of the hand from Dad. He understood there was a kernel of truth in his popular image of a suave cocktail crooner with a devil-may-care attitude. It was the veneer that covered his personal life, which he guarded zealously. But over time, that exterior shell would meld with the grain of his inner self, and for some observers, the two would be almost impossible to separate and corroborate. Invariably, the need to somehow categorize Dad and what made him tick would end in a shopworn explanation that behind the façade was the Dean Martin nobody knew.

Dad did not take himself seriously. I suspect that always perplexed the people who chronicle the fortunes and misfortunes of celebrities, pushing them to find reasons why he did not seem to be the least bit self-absorbed or obsessed with polishing his image. A few concluded that, at his core, he was empty. Maybe that's the downside of not being too full of yourself. Some people assume you must not care about yourself. And if you don't care about yourself, then you probably don't care what people think about you either. So Dean Martin must not have given a damn about any of it, after all, they conclude.

Let them believe that if they want. I always had a sense that the people who were fans of Dad's singing, movies, and stage acts didn't need a pop-psychologist couch trip to figure the guy out, if they even felt a need to ponder such things. It was simple. He liked to have fun. If he was paid for having fun, all the better. It's a credo I've tried to live up to.

His outlook was carefree, rather than void of caring. As his son, I knew this more than anyone. Dad cared deeply about many of the people whose lives intersected with his during his long career. Especially in those last days, after work was no longer fun and life had become all too serious, he would talk frequently about the old days and the friends that peopled his past.

He and I would sit over dinner, usually in one of his favorite Beverly Hills haunts where other customers seemed to be as shocked to see him as much as he was surprised they still knew who he was, and there would be a certain rhythm to the evening. The stories would unwind in an almost predictable pattern: the set-up, the punchline, and then the segue into the next yarn.

Not all of the tales had happy endings, just as not all memories are good ones. But there was a catharsis to the storytelling, a salve that seemed to ease the unspoken sadness that he was slowly dying. I believe Dad was resigned to his fate, and death did not come as a surprise to him or to those of us who had watched his health and desire decline. Still, the death of a loved one, no matter how expected or anticipated, is always a blow. I miss him deeply.

But he always will live on in my memories and in the memories of those who enjoyed his company, whether it was from a song on a phonograph, a seat in a movie theater, a table at a Las Vegas showroom, or in the living room of America every Thursday night on television. It's to his memory that this book is dedicated, even if he was never much for sentimentality.

I can hear him now: "Thanks, pallie, but why'd you do that?"

—Ricci Martin

that's amore

chapter 1

Home in the Hills

The Hamburger Hamlet squats below a glassy medical office tower at a three-way intersection on Sunset Boulevard in West Hollywood, a bygone shrine to fried food and gooey desserts amid the procession of sushi bars and patisseries that line the Sunset Strip. It opened in October 1950 as the "Coffee Shop to the Stars," a little café at Doheny and Sunset with red awnings and a patio that offered "simply marvelous food and drink, prepared and served by nice people." Because the owner was a contract actor and the place was situated on the commute home to the storied mansions in the Hollywood hills, Hamlet fare was routinely carried away in grease-stained paper bags by the likes of Tony Randall, Janet Leigh, and Debbie Reynolds.

But perhaps its most famous regular was my dad, Dean Martin, an Italian immigrant's son who ascended to pop culture icon as a singer, movie star, and Las Vegas stage performer. It was there, in the Hamlet's eternally dim tap room on a Sunday evening forty-five years from the day the place had first opened, that I saw Dad alive for the last time.

I will remember that evening as one of the saddest of my life. After dinner with him, I went to my mother's house in nearby Beverly Hills with tears in my eyes. Less than three months later on Christmas morning, 1995, after a late-night marathon gift-wrapping session at my own home in the mountains of Utah, I got the phone call informing me that Dad had died of respiratory failure.

In my grief, I was glad we had been able to share that last evening together in October 1995. But the final image I have of him sitting in that big, red button-tuck Naugahyde chair at his usual table at the Hamlet is not a pleasant one. When my mother had called and said I should come and visit Dad soon, she had warned me to be prepared when I first saw him.

It had only been a few months since he and I had last met. But his skeletal appearance on that evening at the Hamlet was shocking. He had shrunken from the athletic man I had grown up with, his normally taut body frail and his skin seeming to drape over his frame like a shroud. His thick, black-rimmed eyeglasses slipping off his nose seemed to envelop his small face, once lean and tan yet now pale, even yellow under the low-wattage bulbs sprouting from the brass chandeliers in the lounge.

Neither one of us talked about his failing health, choosing instead to reminisce. He shook his head about the death of another Hamlet regular, Elizabeth Montgomery, his co-star in the 1963 film *Who's Been Sleeping in My Bed?* and the actress who immortalized *Bewitched*, the ABC-TV comedy that jostled with NBC's *The Dean Martin Show* for top ratings in the late 1960s. She had died just five months earlier, on May 18, 1995, of colon cancer. She was 62 and, like Dad, had withered with the passing of time. Talk of her death compounded the sadness of our evening together, weighing on my father like so many heartaches of the last years.

It was only a few blocks up Doheny Road from this dreary last supper that I had forged many of the happiest memories of my life, growing up as the son of this famous man who now seemed to be dematerializing before my eyes. The Martin family home, at 601 Mountain Drive in Beverly Hills, was the center of my childhood galaxy. Two decades of memories radiate from that place like the corona of the sun, concentric reflections of the past that warm me with colors, smells, sounds, and sights of the past.

The purr of Dad's car up the driveway, bathed in alternating bands of the late afternoon light and shadow, and as it rumbled through the carport next to the laundry room and into the garage, the doors of which were always left open. The rhythmic click-click-click of his boots as he entered the kitchen from the back door. I'd be seated at the kitchen counter and he'd walk over, give me a pinch on the neck and the standard greeting that needed no answer, "Whaddya say, pallie?"

He would go over to the bread drawer and pull out a loaf of soft Weber's white bread. Smearing a slice with butter, he would fold it in half and take a big bite off the end. "Now that's livin', pallie," he would announce as he headed up the stairs to his bedroom to clean up for dinner. Coming back downstairs, he would sit on the couch in the living room, smoking a cigarette, sipping a cocktail, while alternately listening to our reports of the day's doings and idly searching the television channels for a western. The picture of contentment.

The evening ritual of his arrival remains one of the most comforting moments of my life. The sinuous path that time followed from those "Dad's home!" hugs of the 1950s to our final embrace before he climbed into his car and was driven away from the Hamlet that night in the fall of 1995 is the story of this book.

If you were to trace my father's lineage forward from his ancestors, family, birth, and childhood, it's unlikely you would expect the trail to lead to Beverly Hills, California. That Dean Martin, a man whose celebrity appeal was rooted in a charming lack of pretension, would make his home in the epicenter of status symbolism was one of the many ironies I came to recognize growing to adulthood.

Dad was named Dino Paul Crocetti (pronounced "crochetty") when he was born June 7, 1917, in one of the oldest communities in Ohio, a town called Steubenville. The steel-mill burg across the Ohio River from West Virginia was named after Baron Frederick William von Steuben, a Prussian soldier who trained the militiamen of the American colonies in the Revolutionary War. Its residents mixed heartland patriotism with scraped knuckles and a dirt-under-the-fingernails work ethic. And at the end of the day, they knew how to have a good time.

Dino was the second son of a barber who came to America in 1913 from Montesilvano, a small town on the calf of the boot of Italy, nestled on the coast of the Adriatic Sea. I don't know if my grandfather, Gaetano Crocetti, ever became accustomed to the fame and fortune that would befall his son Dino. Pop, as we called Guy, was a simple man who enjoyed his family and his ravioli, the latter always homemade by my grandmother Angela. She and Pop were married in 1914, a year after his ship from Italy docked at Ellis Island. He was 20 and she was 16 on their wedding day.

Guy and Angela would occasionally come and stay with us on the weekends at the big house in Beverly Hills. About one Sunday a month, Angela would make an Italian feast at our home with homemade ravioli, sausage, and gnocci, filling the kitchen with delicious smells.

I remember one evening, shortly before his death in 1967 at age 73, Pop announced he was ready for bed. I was asked to help Pop to his designated guest room at the end of one of the wings of the house. By that time, our home had sprawled from the original fieldstone and wood dream house of about 5,000 square feet that Mom and Dad had bought in 1954 for $120,000 cash, to a 12,000-square-foot manor. A second-story extension had been added over the garages for a separate wing of bedrooms for the girls. As I led Pop down the long hallways, he frequently wanted to veer off into one of the already occupied rooms.

"No, Pop, this way," I would say, tugging at his arm to correct his course.

Opposite: Dean at 17.

Previous spread: Lost in space. The Martin digs at 601 Mountain Drive in the early 1960s, after Mom and Dad added on a new wing and tennis court.

Finally, exasperated, he called a halt and asked me, "What room number am I in?"

In spite of its size, we never thought of 601 Mountain as a mansion, but more as a ranch house, harking back to the days not that long before when Rodeo Drive was pronounced Ro-dee-oh, not Ro-day-oh. The L.A. Basin floor of Beverly Hills was once a field of lima beans, and the gently undulating foothills rimming Coldwater, Franklin, Benedict, and Higgins Canyons were planted with wheat, or grazed by cattle or sheep. As the city became the preferred address of movie stars—spurred by Douglas Fairbanks and Mary Pickford's "Pickfair" estate in 1919—the farms gave way to beautiful mansions, architectural wonders of elegance and ostentation.

Farmhands used to herd cows, sheep, and horses down Santa Monica Boulevard, and the bridle paths that crisscross the city used to be dirt, not grass. They were horse trails rather than jogging paths. Even in the late 1950s, with a population just less than 30,000, the town retained that rural flavor. We would ride our Stingray bikes to Morley Drug Co. on the corner of Beverly Drive and Santa Monica. Nearby was Birdsal's, the store where we were outfitted in uniforms for Beverly Hills Catholic School, just off Wilshire.

It was a town where everybody seemed to know everybody else, or knew someone who did, which made it very hard as a kid to get away with anything without a concerned citizen filing a report with Mrs. Martin.

I was just a year old when we moved into 601, and at the time, most of the two-and-a-half acres of grounds were covered with a grove of unkempt orange trees, a dark jungle that created a canopy beneath the taller palm, acacia, eucalyptus, and pepper trees. The house was built on the brow of a hill above Sunset

Mom and Dad were married August 26, 1949.

Boulevard, just below Greystone Park, at the junction of Mountain and Loma Vista.

After their marriage in 1949, my father and my mother Jeanne (pronounced as in "I Dream of . . .") had lived in Los Angeles' Westside before settling into the house at 601 Mountain in 1954, which would be home for nearly two decades. The place was big from my earliest recollections and seemed to grow as the family did.

In spite of the celebrity circle that swirled around my father and mother, the heart and soul of our house were shielded from the glare of Hollywood. When Dad got full custody of my brother Craig and sisters Claudia, Gail, and Deana from his first wife, Betty, we grew larger and closer as a family.

Growing up, I never considered any one of them a "half," as in half-brother or half-sister. Even much later, when Dad and Mom divorced and he remarried, adopting his new wife's daughter, Sasha, I never referred to her as my "step-sister" or my "adopted" sister. Through three marriages and eight kids, we were always one family. The Martins.

Dad had married Betty—her full name was Elizabeth Anne McDonald—in 1941, while he was climbing the ladder as a crooner, singing at nightclubs around Ohio. They had four children: Craig, born in 1942; Claudia, born in 1944; Gail, born in 1945; and Deana, born in 1948. Their marriage was faltering when Dad met my mother, Jeanne, on New Year's Eve 1948. Dad and Betty were divorced a few months later. After Mom and Dad's marriage, our family at 601 Mountain quickly grew to include three children: my older brother Dean-Paul, who was born in 1951; myself, Ricci, born two years later; and my younger sister, Gina, born in 1956. Mom insisted that Dad seek full custody of his four children by Betty, and in a court request, she pledged to raise them as her own. In 1957, a judge granted Dad's petition for full custody. When Craig, Claudia, Gail, and Deana came to the house, they were my brothers and sisters. That's just the way it

Dad was granted custody of my brother Craig, and sisters Gail, Deana, and Claudia in 1957, putting the entire Dean Martin family under the same roof.

was and, seemingly overnight, we coalesced into one boisterous herd of kids.

Today, the popular term to describe us would be a "blended" family. But my brothers and sisters and I never made any distinction. Dad was Dad, Mom was Mom, and the big house at 601 was home.

As you walked into the house at 601 Mountain through the big wooden front door, you entered a large foyer decorated sparingly, dominated by a mirror to the left, an antique with lacy pewter veins in the glass and a ledge adorned with scrollwork at the base. Mom loved antiques and we had several beautiful pieces

The Martin invasion: (left to right) Dean-Paul, myself, Deana, Mom with baby Gina, Dad, Gail, Claudia, and Craig in front of 601 Mountain Drive.

in the house, but the appeal was lost on Dad. He used to joke, "Honey, I make enough money. You can buy new furniture."

To the right of the foyer was the entrance to the living room. This was the hub of activity in our house, whether it was an evening of watching TV, a cocktail party, or a gin rummy game presided over by my dear grandmother Peggy, Mom's mother. More than 30 feet long, the room was divided by a see-through fireplace that separated the television viewing area from the sunken terrace bar that looked outside over the tennis court.

Walking into the living room, you would see the back of a chair that faced the sunken bar, while along the right wall was the couch where Dad would always sit to watch television. His spot was at the left end of the couch, next to an end table that always had an ashtray and a coaster for his drink.

In front of the couch was a small, low coffee table, and if you walked past the coffee table, you would reach three wide stairs of terrazzo, polished marble chips set in cement, that led down to the lower level and the curving bar. The wall at the end of the room was floor-to-ceiling picture windows and sliding glass doors, looking out behind the bar onto a terrazzo patio framed by large planters and the tennis court fence just beyond.

There was a spinet piano in the bar area, used by guests and us kids, never by Dad. Seating was built into the ledge surrounding the bar area, and a game table with chairs perched in the corner opposite the bar.

Just down the main foyer from the living room entrance was a small door that led into the den. This room was used as Dad's office, although I seldom recall ever seeing him in there, let alone sitting behind the desk. On weekdays a secretary worked in the office, answering the phone.

Most of the calls that came in on that line were for Mom. It was a fact of life that Dad seldom had anyone call him at home, and he rarely used the phone to call out. When he was home, he

Dad showing off his juggling skills in our living room, 1967. Myself, Dad, Deana, Gina, Mom and Dean-Paul.

was incommunicado, avoiding contact with the outside world so that he could relax with the family. Dad was the kind of guy who left his work at the office, and everybody who worked with him knew not to try to reach him at home.

Directly through the foyer was a projection room that doubled as a playroom for the kids. There was a billiards table in the middle of the shoebox-shaped area, between the two L-shaped couches that stretched across the room and the screen on the far wall. The billiards table was situated so that it didn't interfere with the line of sight, and the three lights that hung above the green felt surface were rigged on pulleys that could be raised to the ceiling when the show began. The walls were lined with Dad's gold and platinum records, more than a dozen, in an orderly parade around the room.

Dad was a member of the Academy of Motion Picture Arts and Sciences, an honor that allowed him to vote for the Oscars and also to receive first-run films for his personal viewing. The two couches in the projection room were separated by a large antique trunk that served as an end table. It held a lamp, a telephone, and a metal intercom box next to where Dad would sit. We would all assemble on either side of him and Dad would press the button on the intercom and say, "Roll it, Lowell." That was the signal for the union guy in the soundproofed projection room behind the rear wall to electrically lower the screen at the opposite end of the room and start one of the two huge 35-millimeter, heli-arc movie projectors.

Since it was a true home theater, the equipment at the time dictated that a professional show the movie. Each projector was the size of a 55-gallon drum laid across the top of a stove, and columns of galvanized steel ducting sprouted from the projectors to channel the intense heat outside. The projectionist had to constantly adjust the ivory handle that controlled the two carbon rods feeding the heli-arc to produce the brilliant light, much as a welder has to regulate his torch. We watched most of Dad's later

Myself, Dad, Gina, Mom, and Dean-Paul upstairs at home, about 1956. Mom and Dad's bedroom is to the left and Grandma Peggy's room is to the right.

movies, from the mid-1960s on, in this projection room that, at the time, was state-of-the-art.

His earlier films were less complicated to screen. Before the living room was enlarged to include the sunken bar area, it served as our projection room. In those days, the movies that Dad and Jerry Lewis made were rented on 16-millimeter reels. You'd get a catalog in the mail listing the available movies, and they would arrive in oversized pancake tins. The projector was mounted in a closet-sized room behind the wall of the old living room, concealed by a painting that was hinged on one side to swing open when it was time for a movie. I was the one who usually manned the little 16-millimeter film projector for those early black-and-white shows, and while I pined for a chance to fire up the monstrous heli-arcs when those were installed later on, running the two big projectors was off-limits to us kids. Union regulations, I guess.

When Mom and Dad remodeled the playroom and added

the new movie theater system, they also had a low-rise stage built beneath the screen. The stage was used frequently as we grew up, from impromptu family skits and mimicking of Dad's stage antics, to rehearsals for my brother Dean-Paul's band, Dino, Desi, and Billy, and later, for a couple of my fledgling bands.

To the left of the foyer was the dining room, which led into the kitchen and a breakfast nook. A circular staircase wound up to the second floor from the foyer, and directly across from the top landing was the entrance to the master bedroom, where Mom and Dad slept.

Just to the right of the master bedroom entrance was another door, the entrance to a separate, smaller bedroom where Mom's mother, Peggy Biegger, slept. Peggy, my maternal grandmother, lived with us and had as much a hand in raising the seven Martin children as did Mom.

As we kids grew up, we gradually recognized the irony in the proximity of Peggy's room to Mom and Dad's bedroom. Dean Martin was portrayed around Hollywood as a rakish Casanova, winning the charms of beauties from Marilyn Monroe to Ursula Andress. Few would imagine he slept with his wife one wall away from his mother-in-law.

It was not the stereotypical son-in-law/mother-in-law relationship. Dad had a deep, abiding affection for Peggy, a bond that was as close as with his own mother. She had the same refined features that had made her daughter a beauty queen, although Peggy's hair had a deeper strawberry tint than the golden blonde of my mother's hair. She adored Dad and he would regularly do several minutes of shtick about her in his stage act in Las Vegas.

The routine would usually begin with him picking up a drink from a table of an audience member seated closest to the stage. This was a pre-arranged gag, with the waiter usually bringing his scotch-and-soda out to the table of guests right before the show and telling them that it was Mr. Martin's drink for the opening of his show.

Dad and Mom on a date in the early 1950s with Mom's mother, Peggy, who was one of Dad's biggest fans.

Dad would saunter out, do his opening song, and then scan the room, asking, "So, does anybody have a little drinky poo for me?" He would lean over the designated table, swipe the drink, and take a sip, much to the surprise of the rest of the audience, who didn't realize the drink was a prop. Then he would offer a sip to Kenny Lane, his longtime pianist, who would politely decline. Dad would badger Kenny a little, reminding him that Prohibition had been repealed, then place the drink on the piano and turn back to the audience to begin his next song.

Just as Dad would turn around, Kenny would chug the drink, bringing guffaws from the audience. Dad would wheel around, retrieve the empty drink, pluck a lemon twist from the glass and ask, "Don't the band want none?"

Then he would launch into a series of drunky jokes, including a few about Peggy.

"Oh, Jeanne's mother Peggy lives with us and Peggy is an amazing woman," Dad would say. "She's 80 years old and she doesn't need glasses. She drinks right out of the bottle."

It was about twenty minutes of his show, the whole routine that began with snatching the drink from the audience. One night, however, there was a minor problem. I had gone to see Dad's show with some friends and we had gotten the designated drink table, right up at the front of the room, so close you could rest your elbow on the edge of the stage. I was with Spencer Segura, the son of tennis star Pancho Segura. Spencer was a little nervous being so close to the stage.

Just before the show began, Spencer reached over and, without thinking, downed the entire drink that had been placed on our table for Dad's routine. None of us realized it until Dad reached down from the stage to pick up the glass, which was now empty. Spencer went white. Dad, a little perplexed, looked at him and said, "Did you drink all that?"

So, the routine with Kenny was gone, but Dad was able to roll with it, throwing in a few extra Peggy jokes to fill the time. "The good Lord played a dirty trick on me this morning," he would say, shaking his head. "I woke up, got out of bed, and was headed to the kitchen when down the hallway comes Peggy in a negligee. Wouldn't you know it, He put the sun coming up right behind her, shining through the window. And, boy, you didn't want to look. It was like a pair of two irons coming at me."

Farther down the hallway from Peggy's bedroom at 601 were the bedrooms of all the kids and the back stairway, which led down to the kitchen and out the back door to the carport and three-car garage. The lawn sloped gradually down into the orange grove (which later became the tennis court), a wonderful if not scary place to play hide-and-seek and war.

There also were some small pomegranate trees in the backyard. I remember in 1962, during the height of the Cuban Missile Crisis, Mom and Dad sat us kids down and told us that we might

Dad might swipe more than a drink from a stageside table at times. Mom and Dad at the Sands Hotel and Casino in Las Vegas after an onstage cake fight with the Rat Pack.

have a nuclear war and we should be prepared to head down to the basement in case of an attack. I remember going out and picking pomegranates from the trees, to stockpile for the nuclear holocaust. Just trying to do my part for civil defense, I guess.

While the front of the house was not fenced, the backyard was surrounded by a 4-foot-high chain-link enclosure, concealed by a thick growth of hedges, shrubs, trees, and flowering bushes. The carport was on the west side and the tennis court was to the east, along the Loma Vista edge of the property.

There was an entrance to the front of the house from Loma Vista, but no one ever used that steep driveway, instead using the driveway on Mountain that led into the carport. If someone did pull into the Loma Vista entrance, they immediately gave themselves away as strangers to this house. We always parked our cars

In the pool at 601, 1958. Dad with Gina on his back, Mom, Dean-Paul, and Deana. (Allan Grant photo)

behind the house, while guests used the parking area in the front.

In the middle of the backyard, placed against the far northern edge of the property, was the swimming pool with a slide and a diving board. In the temperate clime of Los Angeles, a pool is a must for kids. At first, since we had never had a house with a swimming pool, Mom and Dad tried to discourage us from using the pool without their direct supervision. They erected a temporary, 10-foot-high fence around the perimeter, which we readily scaled.

Soon, after the parental lecture on water safety, the fence came down and we endeavored to use the pool year-round. In Beverly Hills, the only clue we had that winter had come was the Christmas lights strung along Little Santa Monica Boulevard and the twilight that descended at 5 P.M., drastically shortening the days.

Especially during summer vacation, the noise of screaming kids erupting from the Martin pool must have sounded like cats on fire. There were seven of us and we usually invited friends over, creating a collective mass of adolescence that hit the water like the starting gun of a triathlon.

The weather was warm, school was out, and the pool-house

fridge was stocked with Delaware Punch. Kids would come and go like flocks of birds, with Mom periodically peeking out of the sliding glass doors of the projection room to casually check on the level of activity.

I remember late one summer afternoon, when I was probably 10 or 11. I had spent most of the day playing with friends in the pool. The crowd had been upwards of two dozen kids and teens, but as it thinned, my parents noticed one young man who seemed a bit older than the rest of the kids, sitting poolside in a chaise lounge, relaxing. At first they weren't suspicious, because so many kids came and went during the day, and this guy might just be a boyfriend of one of my older sisters' friends. Eventually, Jeanne started asking my brothers and sisters if they knew this particular young man, who seemed a little overdressed, in slacks and shirt, for an afternoon poolside.

None of us had any idea who this person was. "I thought he was your friend," we echoed each other. It turned out he was a fan of Dad's who had driven by the house, heard the ruckus, came through the gate, and just pulled up a chair on the deck. When the police came to escort him out, he didn't protest, looking pleased about how he had spent the afternoon.

Other uninvited guests came with Dad's growing stardom. Early one morning, at about 3:30 A.M., we were rousted from bed by pounding on the front door and a male voice shrieking, "Dino! Dino! Come on down, I gotta talk to ya! Hey, Dino!"

After determining that it was not Frank Sinatra, Dad told the guy to get lost. When the visitor refused, saying he needed to talk to Dad about something important, Mom called the police. The cops learned the man had walked away from the mental ward at the veteran's hospital in Westwood and had apparently hoofed it clear up to Dean Martin's house to hash out some unknown burning issue with Dad at four in the morning. Dad told the police he did not want to press charges—if they wouldn't mind giving the guy a ride back to Westwood.

Another indication that the times were changing came one night when Mom and Dad were watching KTLA, the local television station. The channel aired a sort of Los Angeles version of *America's Most Wanted*, showing mug shots of the most serious criminals from L.A. that police were searching for. Lying in bed, watching the rogues' gallery, Mom and Dad were stunned when one of the criminals on the lam turned out to be a cook they had hired.

A driver they had employed pleaded with them to buy him a new car so he could replace his old clunker and always be sure of making it to work on time. They bought him the car and never saw him again.

After that, they hired a guy who seemed very pleasant and courteous. He was even nice when they drove up to find his car pulled up at the back door while he loaded bottles of booze from the liquor closet into his car trunk.

Eventually, we got our first security guards at 601 Mountain. If you drive around my old neighborhood today, you'll notice signs on some of the driveway gates and fences that read, "Bel-Air Patrol Armed Response." I can't help but smile when I see those forbidding warnings. The Bel-Air Patrol guards that we had securing our house in the 1960s would have made Barney Fife look like Eliot Ness.

The members of the Bel-Air Patrol back then ranged from long-retired beat cops to fresh-scrubbed rookies, the latter hopeful that a stint as a rent-a-cop would get them a sponsorship to the police academy. Each night they were supposed to patrol the house, but this "patrol" usually consisted of sitting in their car while it was parked in the driveway, just in front of the carport, and sleeping. At times, their snoring was so loud we had to go outside and wake them. Or just ask them to roll up the windows.

Needless to say, the Bel-Air Patrol didn't last long at 601. They were replaced by a couple of dark-haired, wise-cracking Italian guys, Jim Babusio and Joe Bella. It is safe to say neither of these new "personal bodyguards," as they preferred to be called, had ever worn a badge. I suspect they were intimately familiar with the law, however.

Our adventures with private security guards at 601 would one day be reflected in a short-lived NBC-TV comedy in 1985 called *Half Nelson*. Joe Pesci played Rocky Nelson, an ex-cop from New York who moved to Beverly Hills to break into acting but worked as a private security guard for the rich and famous, solving crimes in the process. Dad starred as himself in a recurring role, as Rocky's favorite client and Hollywood mentor.

In the real world, Jim and Joe would certainly intimidate the occupants of any suspicious vehicle that pulled into the driveway at 601, but they were easy going and became more like extensions of the family rather than hired security guards. My older brother Dean-Paul and I became especially fond of Jim and Joe, thanks in part to their willingness to go out and shoot guns with us. This kindness would eventually create many opportunities for Dean-Paul and me to get ourselves into trouble.

While guard dogs were never a consideration at 601 Mountain, we did have a canine companion that possessed dangerous charm. During one of those summer afternoon aquatic festivals in the backyard when I was about 6 or 7 years old, a dog with curly, light blonde hair wandered in and cautiously joined the revelry. A collage of breeds, the medium-sized mutt was easily spooked and cowered when approached, leading us to suspect the dog might have been kicked or abused.

Still, the little pooch seemed to like being around us kids and he began to make regular appearances, staying longer each day. Eventually, we learned he belonged to a family three houses up the road, quite a stretch, given how most of the houses then were built on two- to five-acre lots.

Soon, the dog refused to leave our house, forcing the kids who owned him to make a nightly pilgrimage down to our house to fetch him. Each time they retrieved the reluctant animal, my siblings and I became more upset. At this time, we had no pets and had grown attached to the dog. We had come to believe he was better off with us than with the people up the street.

Finally, one evening we convinced Mom and Dad to grant the dog asylum at our home. We took him inside, named him Pierre, and closed the door. When the kids from up the street came to get him, we told them no, he didn't want to go home with them and was staying with us from now on.

A few days went by and Pierre showed no signs of wanting to return to his old home. But one evening, the father of Pierre's former family came to the front door and demanded to get his dog back. He was a towering man, obviously angry that we had shanghaied his shorthair.

We rushed into the living room to plead with Dad to stop this man from taking Pierre, bawling and sobbing that the dog didn't want to go back, he was our dog now. Dad had barely gotten home that evening and I'm sure he didn't need some confrontation with a neighbor as the capper to his day.

He walked to the still-ajar front door, his boots click-clicking across the tile floor of the foyer as we hung onto Pierre several paces behind, tears still welling in our eyes.

The man lit into Dad and accused him of stealing the dog. My father seldom showed anger or raised his voice, reacting instead with a narrowing of his eyes and a calm but threatening tone to his voice.

"That dog is going to stay at this house with my children and that's all there is to it," Dad told the man. Then he shut the door.

The man never came back and Pierre never left. Needless to say, relations with those particular neighbors and the Martins were forever strained. Pierre, however, lived another fifteen years, the rest of his life, at our house as a part of the family.

Captain Klaus was one of the first dogs Mom and Dad owned. On this baby picture of me Mom wrote, "I had to hold 'Cap.' He would have killed the photographer's aid in a second if he came too close to you."

chapter 2

The Crooner and the Kid

A famous French statesman once said that a married man with a family will do anything for money. But just at the point Dad's bread-winning had to cover a wife and seven kids, assorted relatives, in-laws, and a nanny, all under one roof in Beverly Hills, he tore up his guaranteed paycheck and walked away from Jerry Lewis.

I was too young to remember the split, and Dad only spoke of it many years later. When I was born in the fall of 1953, Dad and Jerry were firmly cemented as major celebrities, and my birth as the second son of Dean and Jeanne Martin received a fair amount of publicity in the Hollywood gossip columns and magazines.

The coverage was fueled by Dad's fame—the latest and, ultimately, one of the best Martin-Lewis movies, *The Caddy*, had just been released, as had Dad's eventual hit song, "That's Amore." But it also reflected public interest in whether Mom and Dad were back together for good as the Martin family. Earlier in the year, Dad had briefly moved out of the house after an argument with Mom, an upshot of some of the frustration he was having in his professional relationship with Jerry.

Dean Martin and Jerry Lewis were a Hollywood hit machine, spinning out sixteen films in the span of seven years, beginning with *My Friend Irma* in 1949 and ending with *Holly-*

The Hollywood hit machine, before they landed in the rough.

wood or Bust in 1956. All their films shared two things—they were hugely popular with audiences and were built on the same basic storyline. Dad would play the suave rapscallion in pursuit of romance or riches, only to be done in by Jerry's slapstick bungling and man-child charm. Whether the routine was transposed to Martin and Lewis as soldiers, sailors, artists, busboys, circus workers, or cowboys, it produced big laughs.

Behind the scenes, things were anything but joyous. Dad and Jerry had met by chance in 1946, and many decades later, at one of our dinners at La Famiglia, Dad would relate to me the circumstances of that first encounter. He and Jerry were both playing a nightclub and Jerry went on before Dad, doing an act that involved lip-synching to records that played on a phonograph backstage.

Dad said he happened to be sitting at side stage one night while Jerry was doing his act. Dad looked to his right and saw the phonograph that provided the songs for Jerry to mimic. "Rico, I just took my finger and moved the needle on the record," Dad would grin in telling me the story. "The record skipped and the kid just flipped." Jerry was stunned, glancing back at Dad with a look like, "What the hell do you think you are doing?" But the crowd loved it and Dad continued to bounce the needle periodically through the rest of Jerry's routine, the audience going nuts with Jerry's exaggerated look of alarm at each snafu.

Then it was Dad's turn on stage, and Jerry decided it was time for payback. While Dad was crooning his songs, Jerry grabbed a platter and a towel from a waiter and noisily jostled his way in front of Dad, from one side of the stage to the other, directly blocking the audience's view. Again, the antics left the crowd in stitches.

Opposite: It all started with a skipped phonograph record. Dad and Jerry, the prince and jester, performing in Miami Beach. (Harold Kaye photo)

Afterward, Dad went down to Jerry's dressing room. Jerry was not even being paid for his act at the club, while Dad was earning $50 a night. Dad told me that he suggested that he and Jerry develop a little routine like they had done that night, and Dad would split his $50 with him. Jerry was grateful and they began the classic back-and-forth comedy act that landed them on the very first Ed Sullivan TV show. In 1952, they were nominated for an Emmy as best comedians and won a special award from *Photoplay* magazine for their film work the same year. They were America's funniest duo.

Mom still has a dog-eared clipping of a Hollywood magazine story about our celebrated move into the house at 601. In the staged storyline that was common at the time, Mom and Dad were showing their new home to Jerry and his wife, Patti. There are photos of Jerry clowning around in the closets, sticking his head in the refrigerator, falling over the lawn furniture. Typical slapstick stuff, all part of the Martin and Lewis bag of gags.

But the smiles on the faces of Dad and Mom as they toured their new house with Jerry look strained, giving away some of the tension beneath the surface. Although they ruled Hollywood as bosom buddies—in 1952, Martin and Lewis were rated as the top box-office draw by movie house owners, falling to number two in 1953 and 1954 behind Gary Cooper and John Wayne, respectively—Dad's partnership with Jerry was steadily deteriorating. All the mugging for the camera, trying to show the fans that they were all one big happy group checking out Dean's new digs, couldn't hide it.

Dad seldom mentioned their relationship as I grew up, but not once did I ever hear him speak ill of Jerry. The characters they played in their movies and in their nightclub act seem like a fair reflection of their true selves, opposites to the core.

Dad was self-assured, confident, and although he certainly appreciated adoration, he didn't need critical acclaim to feel successful. He enjoyed making movies, but his first love was singing.

He had followed "That's Amore" with the number-one smash "Memories Are Made of This" in late 1955.

Jerry, in those early years, at times seemed wound tighter than a dollar Duncan yo-yo. Movies were his preferred medium, and Jerry wanted to do films that evoked deeper feeling than the light-hearted comedy of which they were kings. Jerry also seemed to want more warmth and compassion from their partnership than Dad provided. With seven kids at home already, no way was Dad up to being anyone else's father figure.

While Dad was able to brush off Jerry's periodic tantrums, he bristled when Jerry suggested that Mom was coming between them, threatening the future of America's biggest comedy duo. Jerry seemed to be jealous of Mom and resented Dad's desire to spend more time with his family. At the same time, Jerry's ego grew and he began to twist the partnership into a dictatorship.

For Dad, the final straw came in the spring of 1956, when he and Jerry argued about Dad's role in their next picture, over which Jerry had assumed creative control. The standard routine this time would portray Jerry as a lost little boy and Dad as a street cop who befriends him.

Dad balked at wearing a policeman's uniform in the movie, suggesting to Jerry instead that he play the part as a detective and dress in suit clothes. Jerry refused, and he expected Dad to follow his orders, just as everyone else did what Jerry told them to do. Dad would later tell me that he felt it was ironic that their partnership turned to this totalitarian regime of Jerry's, after they had started out their stardom with Dad's offer to Jerry to join his act and split the pay.

Dad turned his back and walked away from Jerry that day, never to work with him on a movie again. There was a touch of an old Italian code of honor in what Dad did, cutting off all ties to someone who has betrayed you in a way that cannot be forgiven. After that, it was as if Jerry had never existed. Dad closed that chapter of his life with a finality that would be repeated only rarely.

Although the common refrain in the entertainment industry was that Martin was nothing without Lewis, Dad ended their partnership without blinking. Jerry made some public criticisms of Dad after their split, and Dad refused to retaliate—except when Jerry went so far as to write a magazine article blaming my Mom for the breakup of the popular duo. Dad had viewed his partnership with Jerry as a business arrangement, not a marriage. He didn't understand why Jerry was launching personal attacks on his wife in public. When a TV interviewer asked him about Jerry's magazine piece, Dad said he felt Jerry had no reason to vent his emotional venom on Mom.

Just like a divorce, the breakup with Jerry was expensive. They had to settle contracts for movies that wouldn't be made and nightclub appearances that would never happen. At the same time, the first of several remodeling projects had gotten underway at 601 Mountain, expanding the house to include rooms for Craig, Claudia, Gail, and Deana.

In the final years of the partnership, Jerry had gravitated toward directing and producing movies, and as a result, he had several offers following his break with Dad, most of which involved grafting a new straight man into Dad's standard role while Jerry continued to play the goofy foil.

Dad, on the other hand, didn't easily fly solo. The first movie he made in 1957 without Jerry, *Ten Thousand Bedrooms*, was a flop. Jerry's lost-kid-and-the-cop comedy came out at the same time and was a hit.

In debt and desperate, Dad agreed to several business deals on the side in the hopes something big would come along to re-ignite his career. He sold his name to a restaurant and bar on Sun-set, which became famous as "Dino's Lodge."

Dino's was frequently featured as the next-door neighbor to the fictitious office used by the private detectives in the popular TV series *77 Sunset Strip*, a show which had regulars cast as Dino's maitre d' and parking-lot attendant. Dad seldom if ever ate at

Near the end, it seemed Jerry was jealous of Dad's attention to Mom and our family. (Barry Kramer photo)

Dino's, and disagreements with the restaurant's partners over the use of his name and likeness as the restaurant was franchised led to a lawsuit, headaches, and regrets over the decision.

The more Dad tried to distance himself from Jerry, the more Jerry seemed to be everywhere. At one time, we heard that Jerry was trying to build his own restaurant across the street from Dino's. Later, when Dad entered the movie studio lot, he noticed an office building under construction. "It's for Jerry," he was told. There was a fancy golf cart, with lights, chrome, and every option imaginable at the studio lot for Jerry to get around.

While Dad had been the singing half of their duo, it was Jerry who scored a top-10 hit in 1956 with a rendition of "Rock-a-Bye Your Baby with a Dixie Melody."

(Left to right) Tony Curtis, Jerry, Janet Leigh, Patti Lewis, Mom, Dad, and Marie McDonald.

Finally, Dad heard Jerry was taking up Dad's favorite occupation—golf. Funny how things work out.

As children, we were oblivious to the clouds on Dad's horizon. If any of it concerned him, it was never manifested at home. He was the same, loving, caring father who had an easy sense of humor. When a Lucky Strike cigarette ad would flash on television, we would ask him what the advertising slogan "LSMFT" meant, knowing full well it stood for "Lucky Strike Means Fine Tobacco."

Taking the set-up, he would explain the true meaning of LSMFT: "Let's Suck My Father's Toes."

Later in life, Dad would pull the same corny routines with his grandchildren. I remember driving in the car sometime in the 1980s with Dad, Mom, Gina, and Dean-Paul's young son,

Alexander, when Dad spotted an airline billboard and explained to Alexander: "TWA: Teeny, Weenie Airlines." Simple and silly. We would laugh and so would he. That was just Dad.

I suspect as with many fathers, playing with his children was a release from career pressures for Dad. One afternoon, Dean-Paul and I each built forts at opposite ends of the backyard at 601 and then filled small plastic bags from the kitchen with flour—"flour bombs," we called them. We squared off behind our respective barricades and began lobbing the flour bombs back and forth when Dad came home. Seeing the exchange underway, he quickly jumped behind my fort, knelt down, and began chucking the powdery grenades. By the time our ammunition was exhausted, we all were covered in flour.

He loved to horseplay and wrestle with us kids, rolling around on the living-room carpet. One of the things I remember most about those times is the smell of his cologne, Woodhue by Faberge. That fragrance, a clean, crisp smell, was a big part of who Dad was.

When we grew older, my brother Craig and I used Woodhue, but it never smelled the same as it did on Dad. Eventually, Faberge quit making Woodhue—Dad and Cary Grant were the only famous people who were using the cologne at the time, and the company had continued making it until Cary's death because he had been a major investor in the company. Craig and I rationed what was left of our bottles and I remember mentioning to Dad how it never smelled the same on me as it did on him.

"That's because you're putting it on wrong," he smiled. He told me to put a couple of drops of water in my hands along with the Woodhue and pat the milky colored mixture on my neck. After fifteen or twenty years of wearing the stuff, I had finally learned the secret of Dad's smell. Later, I told Craig the proper technique Dad had discovered from putting the cologne on while he was still wet from the shower, and Craig said, "Awww, now he tells us." I was down to my last quarter inch of the extinct scent when I learned Dad's technique and have never been able to find the cologne since.

The fragrance was not the only distinctive thing about those afternoon wrestling matches with Dad. While he was certainly able to fend off our attacks—he briefly had been a prizefighter in his youth, nicknamed "Kid Crocetti"—there was one move he absolutely forbade. One day, Dean-Paul put a pretty good head-lock on him and Dad reared up. "Whoa, pallie, not the throat, not the throat," he said. "You see all this?" he asked, motioning to the furniture, the house, the tennis court and swimming pool outside. "Stay away from the throat." We understood the message.

It wasn't Dad's singing that would yield his big break in this post–Martin and Lewis stage of his career, however. He was in a hotel room on Sunset Strip when he got the call that he had won the part of a rebellious soldier in the 1958 war drama *The Young Lions* opposite Marlon Brando and Montgomery Clift. It was a role that he offered to do for less money than any other film he had been in, just to prove he was more than a comedic straight man. It became one of the biggest movies of the year, and critics still call it one of the best World War II films ever made. It was nominated for three technical Oscars—music, sound, and cinematography—and helped legitimize Dad as a versatile movie star, showing that his fans would accept him in serious roles as well as the madcap comedies. He went on to other dramatic roles, in films such as *Toys in the Attic* and *Ada*.

Besides the movie success, 1958 also was a good year for Dad on radio and television. "Return to Me" spent eighteen weeks on the best-selling record charts, peaking at number four. In the summer, "Angel Baby" and "Volare" climbed simultaneously into the top 30.

NBC aired a color special, "The Dean Martin Show," in 1958, the forerunner of what would become Dad's signature weekly TV variety show six years later. And Dad's next movie, *Some Came Running* with Frank Sinatra and Shirley MacLaine,

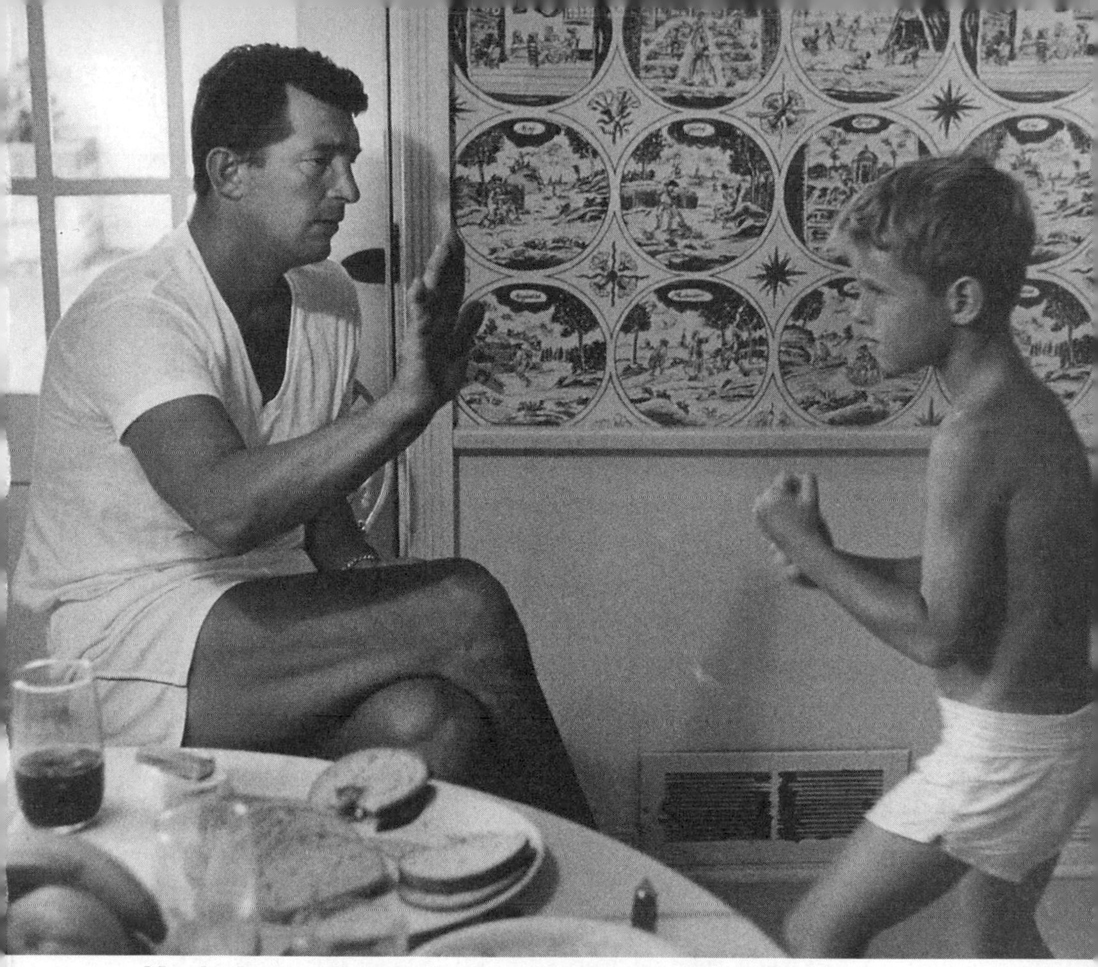

Not the throat, pallie, not the throat. Kid Crocetti coaching Dean-Paul in the kitchen at 601 Mountain, 1958. (Allan Grant photo)

was released in 1958, picking up five Oscar nominations the following year, including a Best Actress nomination for Shirley.

At the edge of the abyss, Dad had built a Golden Gate Bridge. For the next fifteen years he would ride high on his singing, acting, and entertaining talents. Yet with all the demands of his superstar status, I hardly remember him not being home as I grew up. I remember him always being there.

Indeed, throughout the period of Dad's split with Jerry, his struggles financially, and then taking his career to a new level, we remained a nuclear family, insulated from the melodrama and hype. At least until his TV show began in 1965, we all had what seemed to be a very normal childhood.

Not a straight man in the group. Claudia, Gail, and Craig in the back, Mom and Dad in the middle, and Gina, myself, Dean-Paul, and Deana in 1958.

Granted, Dad would go off and do his Vegas show twice a year for six weeks each time. If he had a movie that required him to be out of town, he'd be gone another six weeks. Because of the gallivanting image he had in the early movies and then later crystallized with Frank Sinatra and the Rat Pack, I think people have this image of him never being home. Instead, he tended to treat his stardom as any 9-to-5 job. Actually, it was more like an 8-to-4 job.

Dad was a habitually early riser. We would never see him in the morning, only smell his Woodhue and see the remnants of his toast and coffee—his standard breakfast. For most of his adult life, Dad was up at 6 A.M. By 7 A.M. he was showered, shaved, dressed, had eaten his toast and coffee, and was out the door. Regardless of whether his day called for shooting a movie, recording a song, or playing a couple of rounds of golf, that was his routine. We kids were going to school and had to be to class by 8:30 A.M., so we were rising at about 7:30 in the morning. I believe he enjoyed that quiet moment in the morning, alone in the kitchen, before the house erupted in the hubbub of kids and chores and errands.

We would be home from school at 3:30 in the afternoons and Dad would usually roll in before 5. If he was between Vegas shows and movie productions, he would be golfing. I never knew how he got started playing the game, but he loved it. If it was rainy—which was rare in Beverly Hills—he would play gin rummy with his friends at either the Bel Air or Riviera Country Clubs.

Invariably, though, he would be home for dinner, abiding by Mom's request that the entire family eat together. Dad would come into the house, grab his bread, go upstairs and shower, and be down for dinner around the big table in the dining room.

By now, my brother Craig, Dad's oldest son, had moved out of the house to join the military and was stationed in Germany. As we had grown up, the house had grown out. Dean-Paul and I moved into the bedroom of the three older girls, Claudia, Gail, and Deana, who had moved to their new wing over the garage. Our old bedroom was remodeled for Gina. At one point, I relocated my bed to the hallway outside of Gina's bedroom for about two years, after my frustration with Dean-Paul ordering me around. This was in the days before television remote controls, and somehow he thought it was my job to change channels.

Mobilizing six children from such far-flung confines was always an act of persistence on my mother's part, but she managed to assemble us each evening around the table, where Dad would be seated at the head.

He certainly didn't preside over dinner, however. He used to mutter to Mom during dinner, "Not a straight man in the group," as we would tease, rib, and cut up, a juvenile version of one of Dad's later celebrity roasts. There was a lot of goofing around and Dad would observe, "Too many chiefs and not enough Indians."

Those nightly dinners of us entertaining Dad with impromptu one-liners were probably not that much different

Easter at the Palm Springs house with Grandma Peggy, Dean-Paul, and myself, about 1959.

from the act that he and his other, older "pallies"—Frank Sinatra, Sammy Davis Jr., Peter Lawford, and Joey Bishop—were perfecting on the stage of the Sands Hotel and Casino in Las Vegas.

During Dad's twice-yearly engagements, there were times when Mom packed us all up and took us to Las Vegas. It was one of the few places we ever went as a family, besides Palm Springs. We spent every Easter in Palm Springs, at a house Mom and Dad bought in 1954 for $40,000. It was a quaint cottage that came completely furnished—to this day, Mom still has the vintage pink blender that came with the house. Trips to Vegas and Palm Springs were the only family vacations I remember. We never visited Dad's hometown in Ohio or Mom's former home in Florida, simply because most of their families had moved to California to be near us.

Although my Mom and Dad had spent their honeymoon on the Strip, she told me in later years that she loathed Las Vegas. She didn't mind having the family all together while Dad worked his routine on the showroom stage at the Sands and later the Riviera each night, but in those days, there was absolutely nothing to do in Las Vegas if you didn't golf or gamble.

For kids, Las Vegas was painfully boring. There was always tennis—Dean-Paul was an excellent player and later turned pro—but chasing the ball across a clay court in the searing Las Vegas afternoon was an invitation to heatstroke. Sure, there was a pool, but we had a pool and a tennis court at home, so the novelty quickly wore off.

The hotel had room service, and because of Dad's top-billing status, we could order anything we wanted. But after a couple of days, we tired of that perk as well. The truth was, if you weren't working in Las Vegas, it wasn't much fun.

Dad, naturally, seemed to be having a lot of fun while he was working. As if by accident, the Rat Pack conquered Vegas, epitomizing an era and founding a pop culture dynasty in the desert of dimes.

chapter 3

Summit on the Strip

Early in 1957, Dad walked onto a stage at the Sands Hotel Casino in Las Vegas as an audience of some of the world's most famous celebrities and entertainment industry tycoons looked on, perhaps a bit skeptical if Dean Martin was going to make it solo. He was onstage alone for the first time since the breakup with Jerry, and this was his coming out party. Or possibly his swan song. Dad would later tell me it was one of the biggest moments of his life.

He was on and off in less than forty-five minutes, and the crowd went through the roof, clamoring for more. That night, the Sands management told Dad they wanted to sign him to a multiyear deal and offered him a lucrative contract to headline the showroom.

It had all come together, the good movies, the hit songs on the radio, and the Vegas performances. Dad started having friends visit him while he was doing the Sands shows, and those subsequent parties on the stage coined an image of coolness that Vegas used as tourist currency for three decades.

I don't think I ever heard Dad utter the phrase "the Rat Pack" in his life. That was more Frank Sinatra's saying, although in later years Frank came to disavow the term and its connotation. Still, it was Frank who found it necessary to organize their get-togethers under some fraternal order, convening what he liked to call "the Summit," installing hierarchy where none was needed.

Dad simply enjoyed the diversion of having a couple of his pallies in the front row or on the stage to liven things up. Maybe the ensemble act was a holdover from the routine with Jerry, but he was not the kind to form a club. It was like Groucho Marx said: "I don't care to belong to a club that accepts people like me as members."

Frank was always the self-anointed leader. There was a saying around my house, and it was delivered with equal parts love and sarcasm: "It's Frank's world; we're just living in it."

At the same time, the only one in the celebrated bunch that Frank couldn't order around was Dad. "Hey, Dago! Come over here to the bar!" he would yell at Dad, using an ethnic slur that was only tolerated coming from his *paisan*, Frank.

"Forget it, Dag, I'm going upstairs to bed," Dad would respond.

Frank had never heard anything like it and he loved it. The insolence! While Dad enjoyed the camaraderie of Frank and the rest of the Rat Pack retinue, he still did what he wanted to do. He ran in the pack, but he didn't run with it. Some people saw that as aloofness and smugness; Frank found it irresistible. He knew that was just Dad's casual indifference.

While their clowning on stage was the stuff of a Las Vegas legend, their backstage antics were more along the lines of fraternity pranks. Mom helped start a children's foundation in the early 1950s, SHARE, for Share Happily And Reap Endlessly. She would raise money each year with a gala dinner, auction, and performance that usually featured other celebrity wives in song and dance numbers. One year, Dad, Frank, and Sammy agreed to headline the SHARE benefit and ended up wardrobing together, using the same dressing room. They wouldn't get dressed until the last minute, to make sure their tuxes were perfectly pressed when they went on stage. Before Sammy arrived, Dad and Frank took a pair of scissors and cut the tips off the toes of Sammy's socks.

Leave them laughing and then you're gone. Dad begins his post–Martin-Lewis career at the Sands, 1957. Lucille Ball, Desi Arnaz, Jack Benny and other celebrities were in the audience for his debut. (Las Vegas News Bureau photo)

Come on up. Frank Sinatra joins Dad and Judy Garland on stage at the Sands as Debbie Reynolds, Lauren Bacall, David Niven, Shirley MacLaine, and others look on. (Las Vegas News Bureau photo)

When the stagehand yelled "Five Minutes!" they started getting dressed. As Sammy pulled his socks on, his foot went right through the end and the sock went up his ankle. Sammy was cursing at Dad and Frank, who were almost peeing their pants as they walked out the door cackling. The laughs would continue all night as they knew Sammy was singing and dancing with holes in his socks.

There is a story, repeated many times, that Dad never wore the same pair of socks twice. It's not true. His socks got washed

and worn again, just like those of the rest of us. The ones he never wore twice were the few pair that Sammy extracted revenge on.

Another target of practical jokes was Mack Gray, Dad's right-hand man, and truly his closest friend. Mack was around Dad as much as anyone and was like a brother, traveling with Dad on the road to Vegas and other club dates or appearances. Before joining Dad, Mack had been a boxing manager and the personal assistant to one of Dad's favorite movie stars, George Raft. Like Dad, Mack was easygoing and unpretentious.

We called him "Uncle Mack," and he was the quintessential favorite uncle to us. Whenever he saw us kids he would motion us over, put his arm around us, and pull out a wad of money that was jokingly called a "Steubenville roll," a bunch of $1 bills folded in

Dad makes his entrance with a pratfall during a SHARE charity benefit show.

half. He would peel a few off and slip the singles to us, cautioning, "Now, don't tell your mutha."

He always carried a manila envelope full of good cigars, and he loved smoking them by our pool, holding a reflector under his chin and soaking up the sun. He was perpetually tan and we loved him, just the sweetest guy in the world to us. He frequently had a few words of wisdom for us boys on his dealings with the fairer sex. (Mack had dated our friend Desi's mother, Lucille Ball, before she married Desi Sr.)

Like the extra cash he slipped us, Mack's sage advice on "duh broads" would not have thrilled Mom.

"Hit and run, Ricks, hit and run," Mack would tell me, offering his own version of love 'em and leave 'em. "Oh, I had a screamer last night, Ricks. She was a noisy one. I tried to put my hand over her mouth to quiet her up and not wake the neighbors, and she thought I was being romantic and hollered louder. Oh Ricks, these dames."

Mack was so laid-back that rattling him was a challenge for Frank, Dad, and Sammy. During those boring hours between golf and stage in Vegas, they would call Mack's hotel room and say, "Mack, it's Frank. Hold on a minute." Then they would put the phone in an ice bucket and throw in a lighted cherry bomb firecracker.

The explosion was deafening on the other end of the phone line. Mack would complain about his aching ears for hours, eliciting guffaws through the night.

I remember seeing some of the Sands shows with Dad and the Rat Pack, but my most vivid memories of those times were when Dad moved to playing the Riviera in Las Vegas. I don't remember seeing Peter Lawford or Joey Bishop on stage with him, but I do recall Frank and Sammy. By then, their routine was probably a bit more reserved than the tomfoolery at the Sands, fewer pratfalls in favor of more one-liners. They still had fun together, but as their families grew and they got older, they didn't clown the way they used to. Dad certainly never forgot those great, great times.

Of course, weaning Frank from his hey-hey ways was easier

Uncle Mack taking it all in stride. Tony Curtis, Eddie Fisher, Sammy Cahn, Dad, Frank, and Martin Tannenbaum giving Mack Gray (seated) the usual hard time at the Brown Derby.

said than done. Dad once told me how he and Frank were playing at the Riviera and Frank, true to form, had done it up big. For their dressing room, Frank had taken over a palatial suite of rooms in the hotel, a high-rollers' penthouse complete with a bar, food, and enough room for the entire Rat Pack entourage. "Fun with everything, and I mean fun!" Frank would demand long before the curtain rose. The partying resumed in full force after the show, sometimes until dawn.

But this wasn't Dad's style. He preferred to hang out in his hotel room and then be called twenty minutes before show time, when he would get dressed. He was then escorted from his room by Mack and the security guard, down the service elevator or the back stairs, through the kitchen and to the stage, where the make-up girl would just touch up his face and hair before he went on stage. Dad used to joke that he had seen every casino kitchen on The Strip.

The first night of the gig, Frank demanded Dad join him up in the suite of rooms before the show, and Dad told me he did that first night. "It wasn't bad, but I had to listen to Frank all night," he complained. Coming off the Riviera stage after the show, he spotted a little utility closet just out of sight on one side of the stage. It was used to store ropes, poles, extension cords, and gels for the spotlights.

Dad turned to Mack and said, "That's perfect for me. Tell Jay to put my clothes and a mirror in there and that's fine for me." Jay Girard, Dad's longtime valet—who was perpetually flustered to the point his toupee was seldom on straight—soon had Dad's stuff moved in. Dad didn't mention his new dressing room to Frank.

The next night, before the show, Frank was up in the suite and Dad hadn't shown up. Frank was pacing around, asking,

---

Opposite: And we get paid for this? Dad and Sammy, driving it home. (Las Vegas News Bureau photo)

The Leader always demanded fun. Dad with Frank at the Sands.

"Where's Dag? Why isn't he here?" So one of Frank's guys, Jilly Rizzo, had to tell Frank that Dad had his own dressing room right off the stage in a little broom closet.

Frank came down to the stage and found Dad getting ready in this little room and said, "Dag, what the hell? What are you doing down here?"

Dad told him that it was too far to walk to that suite upstairs and this little spot off the stage was all he wanted, it was just fine for him. Frank stared in disbelief.

So they did the show, and the next night, Dad got the phone call in his room, twenty minutes until showtime. He and Mack went down to the casino level, and Dad walked to his little dressing room backstage and opened the door.

There was Frank, tissue around his collar, a couple of makeup girls getting him ready, the room full of Frank's clothes and food trays and liquor, and a couple of Frank's guys squeezed into the corners.

"Dag!" Frank yelled. "Where ya been? Make room for Dag, everybody. This is his dressing room too."

Dad just shook his head. Frank simply could not be alone, always wanted to hold court, be the one in charge of the festivities. He was the boss, and to be the boss, you need to have people around to give orders to. Dad, being as passive as he was, rolled his eyes and found a place to sit to get ready. For the rest of the gig, he and Frank shared that little utility closet as a dressing room.

During those Riviera shows, a little bar cart would be wheeled onto the stage, triggering a running series of jokes about what had become one of Dad's trademarks since his split with Jerry—the drink in his hand.

Dad played right along. After Frank would say something like "He's got a tan because he found a bar with a skylight," Dad would explain that he'd hate to be a teetotaler. "I feel sorry for you people who don't drink," he'd tell the audience. "'Cause when you wake up in the morning, that's as good as you're going to feel all day."

While it was true that Dad drank, the drunky routines were an act. On stage, and later on the set of his TV show, Dad usually had a J&B scotch and soda he nursed through the performance. It was almost always a weak scotch and soda. Other times it was just apple juice. I never saw Dad drink a martini, although the martini glass logo was frequently used in his TV show promotions and there have been countless martini bars christened in his honor. I suppose much of the association came from the last name he took, but he was never much of a martini drinker.

He also was never one to preach to us kids about anything, although his attitude about not going on stage three-sheets-to-the-wind came through years later, when I was preparing to go on tour with the Beach Boys in 1977 as their opening act in support of my solo album, *Beached*. Before I left, he came up and said, "Pallie, go out there straight for the first time." In essence, he was saying you can't be smashed or high doing this thing; you have to see what it's all about when you first walk out on stage. It was good advice.

In the era in which we grew up, it was commonplace for Mom and Dad to have a late-afternoon cocktail or two. That was socially correct at the time. It was like the TV show *Bewitched*, where Darrin Stephens would come home, complain about his day, and Samantha would make them both martinis before dinner. In our home, however, Mom was seldom if ever the barmaid. Dad would come home, and after getting cleaned up in his bedroom, he'd ask if I would please go down and make him a J&B and soda. I would always make it too strong, and Dad would go "Ewwww" on the first sip, which now seems funny—Dean Martin grimacing at my drink.

While I've had much more practice at properly "Martinizing" a cocktail, not everyone in our family imbibed. Dean-Paul was never a drinker; he never liked the taste of alcohol, and his demeanor of usually being the one behind the wheel, control stick, or trigger precluded anything that would impair his judgment.

There are good drinkers and bad, and Dad was one of the good. He would be just as calm, loving, and funny at home when he had a drink as when he didn't. There was no difference in his disposition. I never saw him drunk in my life.

But if you were to judge his drinking habits only by his stage act, as most of the world seemed to, you would probably conclude he always had a drink in his hand. The image never bothered Dad; it was part of the game, and gradually, people have come to realize that. In 1998, Joey Bishop, the last surviving member of the Rat Pack, told *Time* that he never once saw Dad, Frank, Sammy, or Peter Lawford drunk during their performances, explaining that the booze "was only a gag." Frank once even confessed of Dad's reputation as a drunk: "I spill more than he drinks."

Other aspects of the Rat Pack image identified with Dad also were exaggerated in comparison to reality. The stage shows and the subsequent Rat Pack movies—especially 1960's *Ocean's Eleven*, the story of a group of World War II buddies who scheme to rob five Vegas casinos simultaneously only to have their loot go up in smoke—gave the impression that these were guys who spent all day and night with a showgirl on each knee, dodging flying champagne corks.

In the early days, maybe there was some truth to that. Dad would hit the tables at the Sands after his shows, because the management loved it. After all, the casinos in Las Vegas are not in show business, they are in the "throw" business, as in throw your money on the table, friend. The shows, the food, the ostentation are all intended to keep you coming back to the green felt jungle. Having Dino sitting with the players at a blackjack table, mingling with the tourists tugging the arms of the nickel fruit machines, keeping the action going, was always worth a little extra in the counting room.

Just a little sippy-poo. All part of the act. Who knew it was sometimes just apple juice?

Dad rarely played with his own money, however. He played with house money, cash the casino gave him to gamble with, priming the pump on the floor. That could be the kiss of death for some performers, because you could lose all the house money and then start losing your own, taking a line of credit against your pay for the show. If you were into gambling, it was like giving heroin to a junkie, but contrary to the image, Dad didn't care much for gambling.

Growing up in Ohio, he had worked as a dealer and a croupier—an attendant who handles the money—in the casino speakeasies during Prohibition, so he knew the odds, he knew the house always has the edge. Outside of the casino management wanting him to be out on the floor, laying down a few bets with house money, he would seldom gamble on his own. He knew better and he didn't need to be seen as a big-shot high roller. It wasn't one of his insecurities.

Besides, gambling in Las Vegas is a social thing, a carnival midway for grownups. After a show, Dad was not interested in being social. He wanted to go to sleep. Frank was just the opposite. The holder of the court wanted the reverie on the stage to continue in the lounge, peppering his pallies with feisty slams, dry comebacks, the hoots and groans cascading above the babble of the bar. And it must go on until dawn. No one dared declare seven out and head for the sack.

Dad was never one to willingly be in the midst of the social rumpus that Frank craved. In all the times I saw him at parties or social gatherings, at our home and elsewhere, I rarely saw him belly laughing or being loud. It was just not his style. If something was funny, he would laugh quietly. He never had to shout to be heard, never was the "life of the party." He wasn't Frank, and he certainly was not like me in that respect. Some people think Jerry must have been my real father.

Usually after a show, Dad's fondest wish was to go to his room, go to bed, and watch TV. Again, he was an early riser for his golf game, so at home he regularly went to bed early—say 9 or 10 P.M. The Vegas shows ended late at night, so Dad was weary and almost fixated on getting to his room to bed, obliging Frank with maybe only one or two drinks before slipping out of the mayhem.

For most of his career, his room was rarely higher than the fifth floor in any Las Vegas venue he played. Dad had claustro-

The Ocean's Eleven *premier parade in Las Vegas, August 1960. Kenny Lane, Shirley, and Dad, with Uncle Mack riding shotgun. (Las Vegas News Bureau photo)*

Sign of the times. Las Vegas, back when more than cigarettes came in a pack.

phobia; he hated elevators, airplanes, and any confined space. He would refuse to get into an elevator in Las Vegas in the old days, choosing instead to hoof it up the stairs. In the early days, at the Sands, the casino had private bungalows on the property, and Dad would stay in one of those rather than in a hotel room. Later, when he moved to the Riviera, they didn't have bungalows so he stayed in the hotel. But he was not a masochist for climbing stairs, so he always stayed in the lowest floor of hotel rooms above the casino. With showrooms, kitchens, convention halls, and executive offices, that was sometimes five floors above the lobby.

In the later years of his life, Dad was able to work out his claustrophobia. As casinos expanded and modernized, the hotel elevators got bigger. That put him more at ease. Airplanes, with very few exceptions, were always one of his most dreaded forms of transportation.

Dad's aversion to raucous partying was even more pronounced at home. Mom loved to throw parties at the house at 601 Mountain. Dad hated them. He would come home after work and be heading up the stairs to get ready for dinner and she would remind him people were coming over for the party. "What party?" he would say. Mom would remind him of the thing, you know, the thing tonight. As much as Dad dreaded the party, he wasn't a complainer—at least not loud enough for Mom to hear—and he would make his slow-paced walk up to his bedroom, knowing it was pointless to argue. The people were coming and the house would be full of them in two hours.

Since 1954, when we first moved into the house at 601, Mom had been building a base of interesting guests and friends who were invited to parties at the house. We seldom had people come visit by themselves, for dinner or drinks. Instead, the parties, especially the big one at Christmas, were sort of reunions of an extended family, anchored by a close-knit group and sprinkled with new faces or ones that would come and go. Our Christmas party at 601 was something everyone in Beverly Hills looked forward to. Beverly Hills was still a close-knit community of entertainers, and the Martin Christmas bash was, no question, the party to go to.

The non-holiday parties at 601, on the other hand, were usually Mom's friends, an assortment of entertainment people, volunteers from SHARE, sports figures, and acquaintances from around town. As her own little touch of class, Mom preferred to make her entrance after a critical mass of guests had arrived, so I was always the greeter, answering the doorbell, showing the guests into the living room. Once things were cranking, people laughing and talking, Mom would come down and make sure everyone felt genuinely welcome and cared for in our home.

Dad would eventually saunter in, dressed in casual slacks or khakis, a V-neck cashmere sweater and a La Coste shirt, the kind now called polo shirts, with the collar always turned up. With his Woodhue cologne and that easy rolling walk, he would glide into the room and instantly everyone realized Dean was here. He had that star quality, that was undeniable, and people were truly in awe of him as he walked in. He would simply say, "Hi, how are ya?" Because these were mainly Jeanne's acquaintances and he didn't know many of them well, he would seldom sit down and have a conversation with a party guest. He was not one to ask questions of other people.

Dad would be clever, but he was not a performer at parties. Everyone who came to one of Mom's parties knew they were not going to see Dean Martin sing and joke the way that he did on stage or television. Dad was extremely reserved. He wasn't anti-social. It's just that, as most close friends knew, he would much rather be upstairs in bed, watching television.

Above all, he was not a chatter. The subject of Mom's parties

---

Opposite: In the court of Camelot. Bobby Kennedy, Dad, Mom, and Audrey Wilder.

Next to golf, Dad always liked sleeping best. With a magazine reporter at home in Beverly Hills, November 1958. (Allan Grant photo)

came up once and he said to me, "Chit-chat. It's not the chat that bothers me, Rico, it's the chit."

After about an hour of making an appearance, Dad would meander back upstairs, put on his pajamas, and go to bed. Mom and Dad's bedroom was right above the living room, however, and the noise of the party filtered right up to Dad. For us kids, the hubbub was muffled by distance—our bedrooms were over the garage and carport area in the back of the house. Mom's parties, which built in a steady crescendo as the night wore on, never bothered our sleep. But the noise kept Dad awake, growing louder as it got later, with guests playing the piano, singing, laughing, having a great time as he tossed in his bed upstairs, a pillow over his head, unable to filter out the racket.

He knew complaining to Mom would be pointless. One night, when the celebrating reached a certain volume and hour, Dad picked up the phone and called the police. He pretended to be a neighbor, complaining about a loud party at the Dean Martin house just down the road at Mountain and Loma Vista. "They're being way too loud over there. They're keeping me awake, so would you please send the police over and tell the Martins to quiet down."

When the Beverly Hills police showed up at our front door, Mom was shocked and a little embarrassed that someone—the officers said a neighbor—had sicced the law on her Hollywood soiree. Things immediately toned down, and the party petered out.

A few weeks went by and Mom had another party, with Dad once again the reluctant host-in-abstentia, doing his grip-and-grin march through the living room, sneaking back upstairs, going to bed, trying to sleep as the drone downstairs got louder and louder. His threshold reached, he called the police again, repeating the irritated neighbor routine, and the cops showed up at the door.

Now Mom was getting angry. She couldn't imagine that the noise from her living room guests could be bugging someone at least two-and-a-half acres away. Still, the police were at the door, asking that she keep it down. Grudgingly, she asked the guests to be a little less boisterous, and the party quickly died out.

The next party, the same thing happened. Things getting too loud downstairs, Dad trying to sleep, he called the police. Barely into his fed-up neighbor impersonation, the police dispatcher interrupted him. "OK, Mr. Martin, we'll be right over."

The police had known all along it was Dad who was calling, tipped off no doubt by the unmistakable voice. It would be a few years before Dad would confess his conspiracy to Mom. Even then, she didn't think it was as funny as we did.

chapter 4

Every Kid Needs a Tank

As the Rat Pack hedonism—real or imagined—ramped down in the early 1960s, Dad settled into a polished groove with his career track, regularly doing movies, shows, and albums, but still leaving time for golf and home. He was doing the Vegas shows and the movies, and he was able to enjoy the fruits of his success, whether that meant a new sports car or just more leisure time. Of course, some of those rewards were like an anticipated Christmas gift that, once unwrapped, doesn't measure up to expectations.

Dad loved nice cars, especially convertibles. That may have been a reflection of his claustrophobic tendencies, but it was probably more due to the abundance of sunny days in Beverly Hills. His love of cars came with the same sort of Old World expectation of loyalty and respect that he had toward his friends and business partners. If there was a betrayal of Dad's trust, that was it. He would turn his back and walk away.

He was not a believer in auto repairs. In the mid-1960s, Jaguar came out with its XKE sports car. It was shaped like a cigar, and the only thing that could catch it was the radio. Dad got one of the very first models, in pea green with tan leather interior. He looked great in it.

But back then, Jaguars were unpredictable cars. There is a story that the same company which built the electrical systems for the early Jags also manufactured most of the refrigerators used in England, which is why the British drink their beer warm.

Inevitably, on his way to play golf one morning, Dad's new Jag stalled, quit, and would not start again. He was stuck along Sunset Boulevard, morning traffic starting to thicken. What exactly happened after this, we were never sure. We never saw the Jag again, and when we asked him what happened, he told us with a perfectly straight face, "It stalled on me so I got out and shot it."

Now, I can imagine Dad shutting the door of the uncooperative car, walking to the front of the XKE, then taking out a gun and, bang, one shot, right through the hood. Like a horse in a western movie that had broken its leg, the car had to be put down.

But I also doubt Dad would actually shoot a gun along Sunset Boulevard in broad daylight. The Martins had some pull in Beverly Hills, but not that much. Still, Dean-Paul and I were never quite sure if Dad was really joking about the Jag's fate. We became especially well behaved as back-seat passengers.

Later, when I was in my teens, a mechanic friend of mine tracked down a special car that Dad had wanted to buy. It was a sleek Ferrari Daytona Spider convertible, very rare and still one of the most sought-after sports cars. You don't see them much, but in the first seasons of the mid-1980s TV police drama *Miami Vice*, Don Johnson drove a black Ferrari Daytona Spider, one of the trademarks of Det. Sonny Crockett in the series. Even though Don Johnson's TV car was just a replica of the famed exotic Ferrari, sports car nuts went into mourning when Sonny's Daytona was blown up at the beginning of *Miami Vice*'s third season.

Dad's Daytona was the real thing. When it arrived at the house one afternoon on the back of a special trailer, it was just absolutely gorgeous. Early the next morning, Dad hopped in to drive it for the first time, on his way to golf at the Riviera Country Club in the Pacific Palisades area. Halfway to the links, the Ferrari died. It would not start.

He called me, and although Dad didn't raise his voice, I

No car would dare make Dad late for a tee time. Teeing off at the Riviera Country Club, 1977.

could tell he was fuming. He told me to tell my mechanic friend to come get the Ferrari and take it back to the seller. My friend could keep whatever profit he had made on arranging the deal, but that car "no way, no how" was ever going to darken his garage again.

Sometimes, Dad's misadventures with automobiles could only happen in Beverly Hills. One night, he took Mom to dinner at Chasen's and they drove his Rolls Royce. After dinner, they came home and parked in the garage, and just as Dad was coming into the house he turned around and looked at the Rolls with puzzlement. It wasn't his car. The valet at Chasen's had given Dad the wrong Rolls Royce to drive home. Just a little mix-up, happens all the time.

Several years later, when Dad was living at his house up on Loma Vista, he bought one of the new Aston-Martin roadsters, not the one made famous in the James Bond films, but a newer model, a beautiful car that cost something like $80,000. At the time, Dad had a house man, a very sweet guy who sometimes took a few too many sippy-poos while on the job.

The house had a looping driveway that ran down along a steep hill covered with big trees, and shortly after Dad got the Aston-Martin, he had his house man move it out of the garage to pull another car in. As he drove the car forward out of the garage, the staffer apparently went to step on the brake but hit the gas instead. (How this could happen, we never were clear on.) The car shot forward like a missile, went off the curve of the driveway, up the mountain, and smack into a tree trunk. Dad's house man was shaken but unhurt. The Aston, on the other hand, was shaken, stirred, and totaled.

Growing up at 601 Mountain in the mid-1960s, we always had a station wagon. This was long before the advent of the minivan, and families would either travel via a station wagon or a step van. One of the dealerships or auto manufacturers would provide a new station wagon to Dad each year for the bragging rights, even though Dad rarely ever drove it himself. Instead, it was mainly used by our drivers for errands and to ferry us kids around.

The station wagons also were the cars we learned to drive with, and, as a result, they received more abuse than a rental car with full collision coverage. I remember how one of our buddies, Jay Judson, figured out a routine to make our Pontiac station wagon backfire. We would put the car in first gear and gun the engine to the redline, winding it up to screaming, and then turn the key off. As the revs cycled down, right before the engine died, we would turn the key again. The gas vapors left in the manifold from the previous revving would ignite, and the resulting explosion created a sound that was deafening. It was our little game to drive around, look for someone walking down the sidewalk, then drive up behind them. Jay would drop the car into low, stomp the gas, turn off the key, wait a few seconds, turn it back on, and then we would watch the victim drop a load in their pants out of pure fright.

Of course, the car could only withstand so much of this. The last time we pulled the stunt, the blast seemed to rattle the windows of surrounding homes. When Jay went to restart the car, we found out why. The muffler and exhaust system had disintegrated into a pile of shrapnel beneath the Pontiac. So we limped the car home, sneaking it back into the garage, and played dumb when the next person got in and started it up to run an errand. "Do you boys know what happened to the station wagon?" Nope, not us, no idea, whatsoever.

In the 1950s, Dad did a series of television commercials for Honda and, as a gift from the company, he received two motorcycles. One was a little Honda step-through scooter that had flared fins on the front, and the other was a heftier S-50, which had a belly gasoline tank and a manual gearbox. Dean-Paul and I immediately claimed them as our own.

I have always loved motorcycles, and have ridden them it seems from the time I could walk. Dean-Paul and I rode the Hon-

A night out on the town. Mom and Dad in the early 1950s.

Faster bikes require longer driveways. I always tried to take full advantage of the 601 Mountain Drive speedway on my Honda Super 90, 1963.

das almost daily, buzzing down the long driveway from the carport to Mountain Drive, onto the street in front of the house, and then back up the steep driveway entrance on Loma Vista. It was our very own Laguna Seca, and it pained our mother to no end that we found it necessary to ride on the street years before we were old enough to get a driver's license.

Over the next few years, we outgrew the little Hondas, not in size but in desire for horsepower. In those days, if you wanted to move into the bigger 500-cc and 600-cc motorcycle engines, you didn't have much selection. We found ourselves spending a lot of time at Bud Ekins Triumph on Ventura Boulevard in the Valley, not only because Triumph was one of the few companies making more powerful bikes, but also since Bud was an accomplished rider who did a lot of motorcycle stunts in the movies.

As we tried out bigger bikes, the triangle course down one driveway, out onto the street, and back up the other driveway remained our proving grounds until, one morning, I noticed a group of workers tearing up the vines of ivy at the edge of the front yard. They steadily cleared a 3-foot-wide path along the streetfront through the thicket of ivy, bushes, and ground cover, dug a shallow ditch, and laid two-by-four forms along each edge. That afternoon, another crew came with an asphalt paver and put blacktop over the pathway, which connected at both ends to each driveway entrance and ran parallel to the street out front. Without any ultimatums, Mom had decided to keep us off the public street by building us our own road. So, instead of blasting out onto Mountain Drive, we just swung onto Martin Drive with our motorbikes, avoiding oncoming cars and traffic cops. It was her understated way of ensuring our safety and still understanding our need for speed. Dean-Paul and I always felt how cool it was that Mom did that for us, without any big fanfare.

Our penchant for faster motorcycles turned toward cars as we hit our teenage years, and Dean-Paul especially grew to be an auto enthusiast, in later years taking instruction at Bob Bondurant's school for race car drivers. And so, long before the public safety advertising campaigns came out encouraging people to buckle their seatbelts for safety, I got into the automatic habit of cinching in whenever I went for a ride with Dean-Paul. If there was a five-point racing harness in the car, all the better. Dean-Paul would drive me to school as if he was competing in Le Mans, and I learned that close calls and minor crashes were part of the ride. It was better to walk away from a wreck than to wind up in a hospital bed.

To be sure, a teenage boy with his own Lamborghini Mura S sports car with the transverse-mounted 12-cylinder engine was unusual, even in Beverly Hills. That mustard yellow car, which I believe is now part of Jay Leno's fabulous collection, cost $23,000 in the mid-1960s when it came out, which was an outrageous amount of money for a car at the time. But Dean-Paul had struck gold at a young age when his pop band Dino, Desi, and Billy scored a string of hit records beginning in 1965, and like Dad, he was entitled to enjoy the bounty of his success.

Dean-Paul's frequent scrapes with immovable objects and

other cars were not so much a result of bad driving. The trouble, I told him several times, was that everyone else on the quiet streets of Beverly Hills did not have the same acumen behind the wheel or the same craving to go bombing down a twisting canyon road. If the chance for a little off-course racing practice presented itself, from a yellow light to a Corvette driver with a bloated ego, Dean-Paul would seize the opportunity.

Even something as mundane as loading our enduro motorcycles onto a stake-bed truck became an Evel Knievel photo-op. Thanks to Mom pulling a few strings with studio executives, we often would get permission to ride our dirtbikes and dune buggy on the rugged terrain of the 20th Century Fox location ranch near Calabasas on the weekends, when no productions were shooting. A security guard would open the gate for us, and we would race around the ghost towns of abandoned movie sets on the ranch. Buzzing through the *Planet of the Apes* movie backdrops, we would pause to act out a few favorite scenes, imitating Charlton Heston: "I am not an animal, I am a human being!"

We'd begin the day by loading up the equipment onto a flatbed trailer and a stake-bed truck for the drive to the ranch. Normally, we would walk the motorcycles up a steep gangplank between the trailer and the higher-clearance truck bed. But one morning, Dean-Paul decided to ride his Triumph 500 up the ramp onto the truck rather than walk it. He had watched the Steve McQueen movie *The Great Escape* twenty-one times and was perhaps suffering from hero worship. Steve McQueen made jumping a motorcycle over barbwire fences to escape the Germans look easy. Actually, it was Bud Ekins who made it look easy in the movie.

This was one of those accidents I could see coming from a mile away. I told him he was nuts, but he was determined. As Dean-Paul was gunning the bike up the plank from the trailer to

---

Opposite: Dean-Paul and myself with Mom at the pool at 601, 1954.

the truck bed, the front of the plank shot up and the bike flipped, landing on top of him as he fell backwards onto the front edge of the flatbed trailer, which was protected with a six-inch-high lip of metal. Dean-Paul fell on his back onto the metal lip and the bike came down on his chest, sandwiching him briefly before it tumbled off. He jumped up holding his back in pain, swearing to give it another try. I convinced him to wait for another day, and we walked his bike up the gangplank onto the truck. Although he never told anyone, his back injury from the failed stunt would persist for years.

That was always Dean-Paul's style—never show fear and use as much horsepower as you've got. Most of the time, it was a strategy that helped him escape serious injury.

There was still a tinge of adolescent invincibility in Dean-Paul that worried Mom, whose admonitions to ride safely were frequently lost in the blare of an accelerating two-stroke engine. Before dawn each day, Dean-Paul would get up and pull on his skin-tight leather motorcycle jacket, just like the one Steve McQueen wore, and ride his dirtbike up into the hills behind our house to Doheny Estates, a new subdivision project. There, before the construction crews arrived, he would practice jumping his motorcycle over the freshly dug basements of future homes, using the mounds of dirt on either side of the excavations as ramps.

Mom knew that the direct approach was useless in trying to get Dean-Paul to be careful. So, unbeknownst to us, she called Steve McQueen's wife, Neil, and asked for a little favor. A few days later, Steve McQueen showed up at our house on his motorcycle, wearing that signature leather jacket, and asked if Dean-Paul wanted to go riding with him. By the end of the day, Dean-Paul had gotten a primer on motorcycle safety and riding skills, whether he realized it or not, much to Mom's quiet delight.

In the mid-1960s, our pursuit of motorized toys at 601 took a military turn. One of my best friends from school, Wayne Tweed, found an old, surplus World War II weapons personnel

Tanks for the lift. Me behind the braking levers of our tank, cruising the family ranch near Thousand Oaks, California.

carrier that was for sale at an auto upholstery shop in Inglewood. It was called a "Weasel," basically a tank minus the cannon turret. It was flat-topped with a windshield, was steered by two braking levers that alternately locked either track, and was powered by a Studebaker straight-six engine.

Wayne knew Dean-Paul was crazy for this kind of stuff, so he told Dean-Paul about this tank that was for sale, for a mere $1,500. Dean-Paul had a top-20 record at the time, "I'm a Fool," with Dino, Desi, and Billy, and he was making good money on his own. He didn't need to ask Mom or Dad for the cash. Besides, Mom and Dad had left town for a few days to celebrate their wedding anniversary alone.

Once he saw the tank, Dean-Paul bought it on the spot, and he and Wayne went to Sam's U-Haul and rented a heavy-duty flatbed trailer and a stake-bed truck to tow it. When the procession pulled into the driveway at 601, it was as if one of our favorite TV shows, *The Rat Patrol*, had just invaded Beverly Hills. I giggled with anticipation. Now this was going to be fun.

Shirley and Frank helping Mom and Dad celebrate their anniversary.

Our first decision was that the drab olive-green color on the armored vehicle had to go. We repainted it a luminescent green, the sort of psychedelic hue that was more commonly seen on a Volkswagen Microbus. Then we pulled the tank into the far-right-hand stall of our three-car garage, right next to Mom's car in the middle spot. The empty lefthand spot was where Dad always parked the car he was driving at the time, with most of the other cars parked in back of the carport. Recognizing the potential parental fallout of finding a military assault vehicle in the garage upon their expected arrival that night, we made up a sign and hung it on the side of the tank: "Happy Anniversary Mom and Dad"

Sometime late that night, after we had gone to bed, Mom and Dad arrived home from their weekend getaway. Dad later told me that he pulled his car into the garage next to Mom's, they got out and walked into the house, up the stairs, and began getting ready for bed.

Putting on his pajamas, Dad suddenly did one of his classic double-takes, turned to Mom, and said, "Was there a tank in the garage?"

Mom rolled her eyes, figuring Dad must have had one too many. "No dear. Goodnight."

The next morning, like clockwork, Dad was up early, had his toast and coffee, and strolled out to the garage to head for the golf course. As he walked to his car, he saw the bright green tank, smiled to himself, got in his car, backed out, and made his tee time. Mom was a tougher sell, of course, but we eventually convinced her to let the tank stay. After all, it was a lot safer in traffic than a motorcycle.

The 3-foot-wide paved pathway she had built for us in the motorbike days would barely contain one track tread of the tank. We drove the lumbering rig down the driveway and out into the street for a spin around the block, which was a 3-mile patrol up Loma Vista, left on Doheny Road, and down Schuyler back to Mountain Drive.

By now, the local police had come to expect the unusual from 601 Mountain Drive. Our tank was not street-legal by any stretch, and one of the officers we knew by name, Fred Cook, would just shake his head as he watched the Martin kids driving their tank around the block in Beverly Hills. Motorists on Loma Vista and Doheny had slightly more animated reactions to the big green machine rattling down the road. People always kindly got out of our way.

We added the tank to our growing fleet of off-road vehicles that were trundled out to the 20th Century Fox location ranch on some weekends. After a time, it became a piece of Hollywood

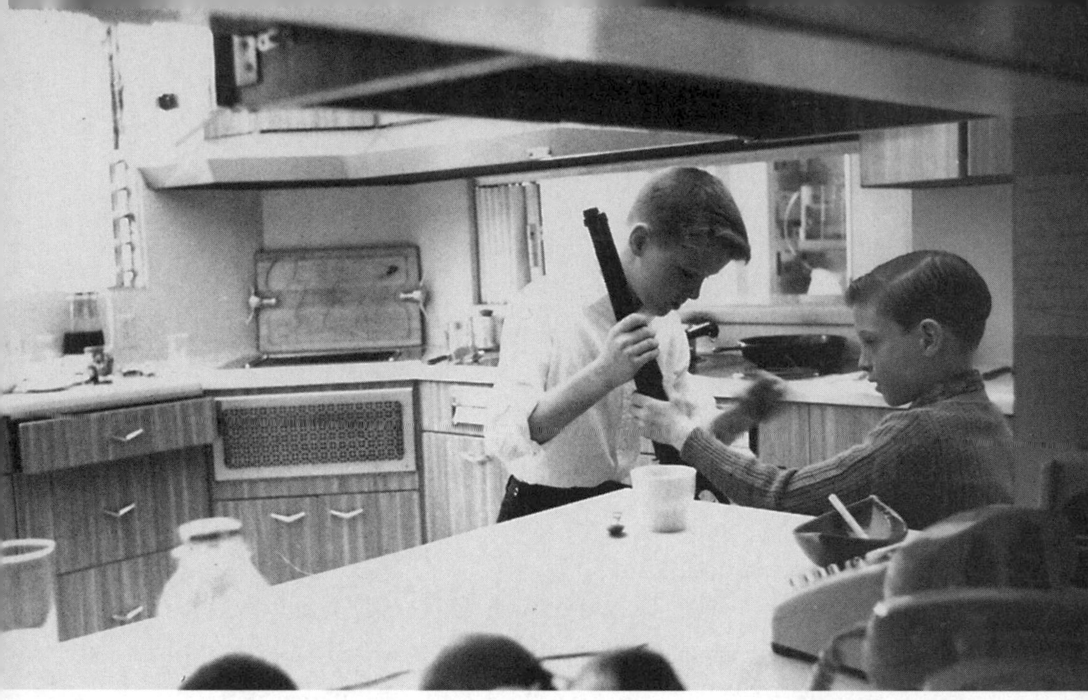

Could we convert it into a fully automatic BB-gun? Dean-Paul and I, searching for targets in the kitchen in 1959.

lore, and people in the entertainment industry would ask Mom and Dad if it was true that their kids had a tank. Several times, Mom would invite friends out to the location ranch on weekends to go for a ride in the tank. Those excursions ended abruptly one Saturday afternoon, however, when Dean-Paul was ferrying Mom and a group of her friends around. They were looking at old movie sets when Dean-Paul came upon a deep, muddy stream, more like a river, and decided to ford it. Once again, show no fear and use all the horsepower you've got.

The tank splashed into the water and was lugging through fine until the water rose to the level of the engine compartment and stalled the Studebaker engine. The iron beast was stuck in the middle of the stream and began to take on water. After trying to restart the engine with no luck, Dean-Paul yelled, "Every man for himself," then jumped overboard and waded to shore. Mom, ever the gracious host, kept her cool and convinced her friends that they, too, must get wet. There were no lifeboats aboard the tank. Fortunately, they all made it to shore.

The next week, the studio had to bring in a crane to extract the tank from its wet, sticky resting place. We were able to repair the engine and salvage the tank. Eventually, we moved it to a ranch that Mom and Dad bought in Thousand Oaks, where it was retired after many a battle campaign down the streets of Beverly Hills.

Our tank commander adventures dovetailed with another hobby that Dean-Paul and I enjoyed, one that Mom and Dad also graciously endured. We liked guns. We always wanted to see what a bullet would do to a tin can, mound of dirt, or stack of milk bottles. My brother and I had collected guns since we were kids, from Daisy BB rifles to antique pistols. The walls of our room were lined with gun cabinets and gun racks, filled with every manner of rifle and handgun. We developed a profound respect for firearms.

Rio Dumbo. Dean-Paul and I loved playing cowboys just like Dad, although I was a little lacking in horsepower. At my grandfather Ken's ranch, about 1955.

The enthusiasm for weaponry may have stemmed from idolizing Dad, who played cowboy gunslingers, soldiers, and secret agents in his various films. Whenever he was shooting a movie that had gunplay in it, he would bring home some of his prop guns and a box of blank cartridges. The three of us—Dad, Dean-Paul, and I—would go out into the backyard and pretend we were cowboys, using the realistic guns to fire blanks at each other. As a parent myself now, I honestly can't imagine doing this today, with the strict handgun laws and society's dim view of guns as toys. But back then, we thought it was just a cool way to play.

It was also a noisy game, but the neighbors and the police had grown accustomed to various bangs and booms from 601 Mountain Drive. If a day or two went by without some sound of detonation coming from our house, then they were worried.

We were very good customers of a local gun shop called the Brass Rail. Big John Hendrix, one of the guys who drove us around, would take us to the Brass Rail and buy ammunition for our plinking trips. The proprietors knew Big John and they let him buy our .30 caliber M-1 cartridges by the handful from big bins. They would count each handful as, say, a dozen rounds, when in fact Big John's hands were so huge he was getting twenty or more rounds. He was the only customer allowed to buy ammunition like that.

As with many of our recreational pursuits, however, Dean-Paul and I probably pushed the gun thing past the limit of Mom and Dad's expansive tolerance. There was the time that Dean-Paul ordered a military surplus 20-mm cannon through the mail. I believe this particular loophole in gun control laws—the selling of heavy artillery to kids via mail order—has since been closed. Now, they can just use the Internet.

The cannon was an anti-tank gun that had been made in Switzerland, a big heavy iron monster that had become obsolete with the advent of bazookas. It came in a specially molded crate and included a sighting scope and a huge magazine that mounted on the bottom of the barrel. It fired 20-millimeter armor-piercing shells, huge cartridges that were about a foot long each.

This wasn't something we could shoot at tin cans in the backyard, so we would take it out to the desert when we visited the house in Palm Springs. Dad would go out with us, and we would find an old rusted hulk of a car for target practice. The holes we left in that car were bigger than grapefruits.

Even out in the middle of nowhere, however, we managed to draw some unwelcome attention. One time, minus our fatherly escort, Dean-Paul and I were reeling off rounds with the AR-15 we had. Dean-Paul noticed a sheriff's patrol car coming our way, so he quickly pulled our car forward to cover the scattering of spent cartridges on the ground and stashed the gun in the trunk.

The officer drove up and asked us, "Have you guys seen anyone shooting around here?" and we said, no, we haven't. Apparently, some homeowners across the valley had heard the rapid fire of the AR-15 and figured they were under attack. Lucky for us, the deputies left without noticing the incriminating pile of brass under the car.

Dean-Paul and I started experimenting with explosives, buying charges that were sold for removing old tree stumps. We nicknamed the smaller bombs "lemonade" because they were the size of a can of frozen juice concentrate, and the bigger charges were dubbed "orange juice," since they were about as big as a quart pitcher. Plus, those nicknames seemed like a natural progression from our "cherry bomb" stage.

Like Dad and his pranks on Uncle Mack, Dean-Paul and I found myriad uses for cherry bombs, the big firecrackers. None of those uses were productive, of course.

In front of the house at 601 was a beautiful ornate mailbox that had been installed at the time the house was built, in 1952. Ivy had grown to cover the mailbox, and it was a manicured showpiece. It also was too tempting as a target. One day, Dean-Paul wondered what a cherry bomb inside the mailbox would do.

During an Air Force publicity tour of Vandenberg, Dean-Paul and I grill the base brass on the possibilities of cherry bomb–powered cruise missiles.

We discovered it would basically blow it to smithereens, along with the ornamental shrubbery around it. Dean-Paul was in big trouble for that, and the awkward, naked mailbox installed as a replacement provided a constant reminder of the bombing for the next few years.

Another experiment involved one of Dad's pipe-smoking friends who was visiting at our house. When he and Dad went into another room, Dean-Paul and I inspected the beautiful, expensive, cherry-wood pipe he had left behind. "That bowl looks like the perfect size for a cherry bomb," Dean-Paul said. He decided to test his hypothesis and discovered, indeed, it was a perfect fit. Now, a cherry bomb inside a pipe is too temping an attraction, so he lit the fuse and vaporized the guest's pipe. The visitor left his pipe at home the next time he came to our house.

Discipline at home, as far as Dean-Paul and I were concerned, basically came from older siblings, especially Gail. While we were growing up, she kept us on our toes, enforcing rules like no elbows on the table, don't talk with your mouth full, and never set the curtains on fire—the usual stuff. The few times we really did something bad and Mom felt we needed a serious talking to, she would send us into the den so that Dad could lay down the law.

I forget what I had done to deserve a trip to the den, but I remember throwing a temper tantrum once I got in the room, tipping over chairs and furniture. The door opened and it was Dad, and immediately I was ashamed of my little fit and upending everything in the room. He walked in, looked around, and said with a bit of surprise, "Did you do all this?" I began crying because I was embarrassed and he said, "Now wait a minute, settle down. Let's put all this furniture back."

We restored the room and sat down. "Now, you know what you did was wrong. You know it and I know it and we don't need to say anything more about it," Dad said. "The thing is, right now we've got to spend about five more minutes in here so your mom thinks I'm giving you a real good talking to."

So we chatted about a few things for another five minutes then emerged, father and son. I appreciated and respected the way he handled that. And I never wanted to put him or myself in that position again.

Lessons are sometimes long in learning, however. One Christmas morning, my grandfather, Ken Biegger, surprised Dean-Paul and me with an incredible wooden fort that he built in the backyard near the orange grove. Nothing was there Christmas Eve, and the next morning, Mom and Dad led us out to the spot to find this big, two-story, wooden Old West style fort, which we loved. After we got older, my younger sister Gina took over the fort and it was transformed into a playhouse, furnished with her play oven and appliances, and occupied by a sorority of dolls. Eventually, she played in it less and less, and one afternoon, still in our cherry bomb phase, Dean-Paul and I decided it was time for a little urban renewal in the backyard.

We rigged cherry bombs in all the corners and at the ends of the load-bearing beams. We lit the fuses and the explosion was deafening. While the fort looked like it had been under missile attack, it still stood, so we descended on it with sledgehammers and razed it to the ground. When Gina discovered the demolition project on her playhouse, she was outraged. She has never let me forget that one.

There's no denying we were reckless at times. My best friend, Wayne Tweed, remembers standing out in front of 601 when Dean-Paul lobbed a cherry bomb from an upstairs window in an attempt to scare Wayne. It did, as well as ripping open the end of Wayne's thumb with a piece of shrapnel. The injury happened so fast, Wayne didn't even realize at first that he was bleeding and sort of brushed it off as no big deal. Dean-Paul, however, was wracked with guilt over the stunt and probably felt worse than Wayne. He insisted on bandaging Wayne's finger and apologized profusely.

Still, we eventually wanted to graduate to hand grenades,

Boxers in boxers. Myself, Dad, and Dean-Paul in the living room at home, 1958. (Allan Grant photo)

which is where Mom had to draw the line. She told us, "Boys, the cannon is fine, machine guns are OK, but absolutely no hand grenades in the house." We were disappointed.

Her concern was actually not so much for our safety, but for the protection of the people who helped around the house and sometimes cleaned our bedrooms. What if Irma, one of our most beloved housekeepers who was considered a member of the family, was straightening a sock drawer and accidentally pulled the pin of a hand grenade? We grudgingly recognized Mom was probably right.

Once I stuck a decal of the German Nazi swastika and eagle crest on my bedroom mirror. Irma, a German Jew, had been in Germany when the Russians came in during the war. She had worked for us for seventeen years, but at the time I didn't think of the connection. When she saw the decal, she admonished me, "Now you take that swastika down or I will not make your bed!" Needless to say, the decal came down immediately.

Dean-Paul and I were very heavy into collecting military

equipment, from guns and tanks to other memorabilia. Even in the 1960s, a couple of decades removed from World War II, it was astonishing what you could buy from the military surplus stores and catalogs. By our late teen years, we had amassed a fine collection of machine guns. Back then, machine guns were a curiosity, or collectors' items, and did not have the assault rifle and paramilitary extremist stigma that they carry today.

Many of the weapons were fully automatic, meaning they would fire bullets continuously as long as the trigger was depressed or until you ran out of ammo. We had a few that were semiautomatic, firing one round each time the trigger was pulled, and I started tinkering with one of the semi-autos, a rifle that looked like the old WWII "grease gun," like a grease gun used in an auto service station. I wanted to see if the firing mechanism could be altered to allow the gun to fire like one fully automatic.

As with most of our brotherly projects, I was the mechanic and Dean-Paul was the designated operator. We used to experiment in the basement of the house at 601, in an area that also was used for storage. After I finished filing away on the gun's trigger mechanism, I gave it to Dean-Paul to try.

I put three cartridges in the magazine and told him to pull off two and release the trigger, so we were sure that it would stop firing when the trigger was not depressed. I didn't want a full magazine of thirty rounds of .45 caliber bullets emptying out of control in the basement.

Understand, though, that automatic weapons fire from the subterranean levels of 601 was not anything the help upstairs would be alarmed over. The maids and handymen were accustomed to seeing dust rise from the foyer floor from the concussion force of detonating large-caliber ammunition repeatedly

---

Opposite: Armed and dangerous. Myself and Dean-Paul, ages 11 and 13. (Guy Webster photo)

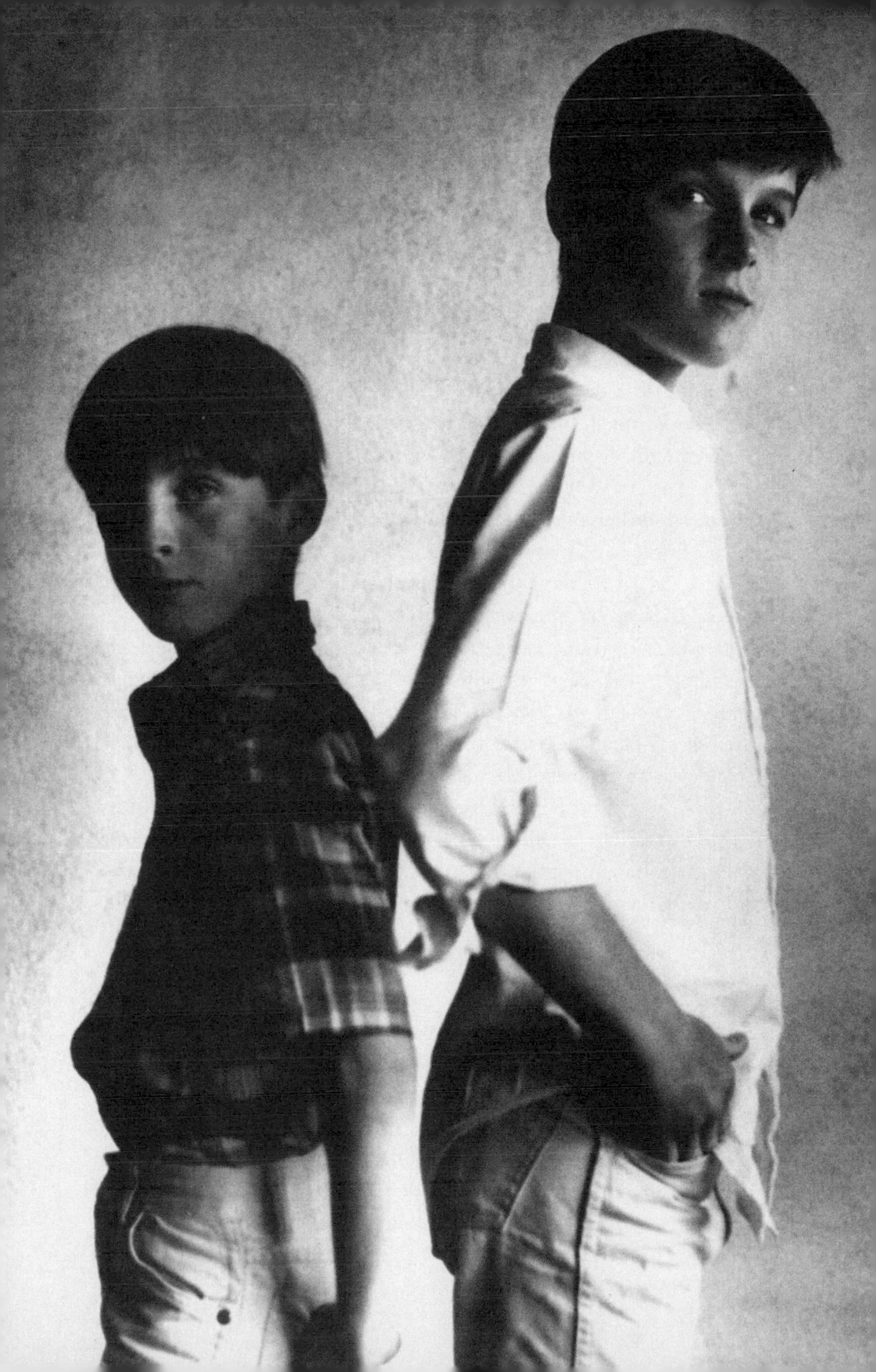

down below. Sometimes, they would even get a whiff of the gunpowder.

Dean-Paul took my modified gun and aimed it at a bag of old rags we had placed against an open section of earthen wall in the basement, a spot we had cleared out between stacks of stuff for periodic test firing. A little skeptical of my abilities to convert the semi-auto into a fully automatic machine gun, he nonchalantly squeezed the trigger and two bullets erupted out of the muzzle. He was stunned. Immediately, we pulled the magazine and loaded it with a full complement of thirty rounds for a complete test.

The trouble with machine guns is keeping the barrel pointed in the same place round after round. The recoil effect of each firing is compounded by the immediate firing of the next cartridge, so holding the gun level is difficult, especially for a teenaged boy. In other words, the bullets started to stray. Not that we noticed right away. It seemed like our bursts of gunfire were landing in the bag of rags in front of the wall. But as the smoke began to clear, we noticed that Mom's cherished set of embroidered luggage stacked to the right of the target zone had been strafed with bullet holes.

We were in deep trouble. About the only people in the house who had a laugh about the little machine gun caper were Jim and Joe, our Italian security guards. After we told them what happened, they dubbed my illegally modified gun the "Steubenville Schmeisser," after Dad's hometown.

Dean-Paul would continue collecting machine guns into his early 20s, and amassed nearly a dozen fully automatic versions, including a German Schmeisser, a Thompson submachine gun, a British Sten gun, an AK-47, an M-16, one of the real World War II "grease guns," a compact 9-mm submachine gun used by the French underground, and my infamous Steubenville Schmeisser.

After he married actress Olivia Hussey and their son, Alexander, was on the way, Dean-Paul realized he ought to get rid of the machine guns. They are not really the things to have around with a toddler. He started selling the machine guns privately to other collectors. This is legal if you have a special permit from the federal government. He didn't.

Dean-Paul had moved into a beautiful house off Benedict Canyon Drive and had taken most of the machine guns with him to the new spread, although I had kept the little French machine gun at home with me at 601, along with the rest of his gun collection. We had a tip that the authorities had gotten wind of our machine gun hobby and were poking around. I took that rumor seriously and I honestly don't know why Dean-Paul didn't. My worst fear was that a bunch of federal agents would be kicking in the door of 601 Mountain to drag me and my bombs and machine gun off to jail.

Before Dean-Paul took the machine guns to his new house, I had wiped down every one of them, cleaning each weapon of any fingerprints. I did the same with the French automatic, removing any trace that I had touched it. I loaded all my lemonades, blasting caps, and explosives into a bag and put the clean machine gun in and handed it over to Jim, one of our goodfellah guards. I told him, "Take this, get rid of it, and don't tell me what you did with it." That was the end of my adventures in pyrotechnics and gunsmithing. It was in the nick of time.

A short time later, Dean-Paul sold two machine guns to a pair of undercover agents from the U.S. Bureau of Alcohol, Tobacco, and Firearms, assuming they were collectors. As soon as he accepted the cash, they pulled out their guns, yelling at him to lay down on the ground, while Olivia and baby Alexander were being told by other agents to freeze.

It was quite an undertaking, with a helicopter circling above and dozens of ATF agents swarming the place. They seized every gun in the house and then took him to 601, where they nonchalantly walked through the kitchen with Dean-Paul while Gina was baking a cake. She assumed the gentlemen were prospective gun buyers, never realizing Dean-Paul had just been arrested.

They hauled all of the guns out of the house, while Dean-Paul gave no hint that something big was going on.

At age 22, he was indicted by a federal grand jury on eleven weapons charges. Dean-Paul pleaded not guilty. I felt heartbroken for him, while at the same time relieved that I had gotten rid of the goods at 601.

As Dean-Paul's trial date got closer, there was growing concern about the competence of his lawyer, who seemed to spend more time grandstanding with the media than preparing Dean-Paul's defense. The case drew a lot of attention because this was Dean Martin's son facing felony firearms charges, but the lawyer kept telling Mom and Dad not to worry. We knew that Dean-Paul certainly did not intentionally break the law and was not some sort of underground gun-runner, but all the same these were serious criminal charges that could mean more than ten years in prison if he was convicted.

Finally, Frank Sinatra called Dad one day and said a reliable source had told him that if Dean-Paul's lawyer stayed on the case, Dean's son would go to prison. Dad trusted Frank and he fired Dean-Paul's lawyer and hired a new one, who told Dean-Paul to face the music and switch his plea to guilty. Dean-Paul agreed, held his breath, and waited for the judge's sentencing. He got a year's probation and a $200 fine.

The judge recognized that Dean-Paul was not a career criminal. But the agents who had made the bust were angry that Dean-Paul had gotten off, blaming the light sentence on who his father was. We had always felt that's why he was targeted in the first place, because he was Dean Martin's son.

After the sentencing, the ATF called Mom and told her that someone needed to come and collect all the other guns that had been seized in the raid. Mom, who was still steamed that Dean-Paul had been treated like a gun-running kingpin by some head-hunting *federales*, asked me to go along with her to make sure we indeed got back all of the guns in the collection. The guns were

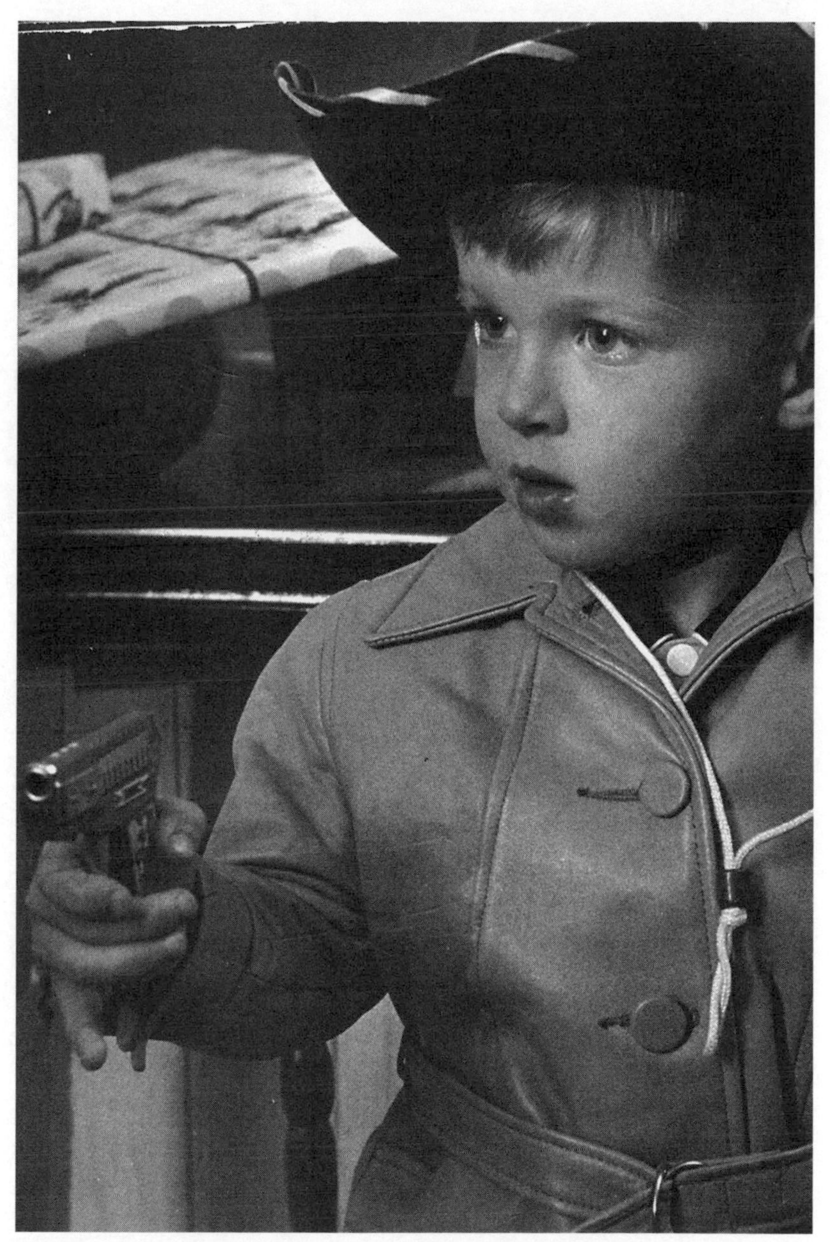

Dean-Paul at his third birthday party in 1954, trying out one of his favorite gifts. The ATF probably had him under surveillance even then.

being held at the ATF offices in the Valley, and we headed over there with Chuck Roven, Dean-Paul's good friend and manager at the time, in Chuck's Rolls Royce.

We pulled up at the address they gave us and it was an office tower with a bank in the lobby. I remember thinking, "OK, there must be a back way in because they aren't going to let us walk through a bank with all these guns."

We went into the bank lobby, over to an elevator, and up to the seventh floor, where the two arresting agents met us in a hallway with a shopping cart. These two guys were obviously pissed over the outcome of their case against Dean-Paul, and they literally threw the guns into the shopping cart as they read through the evidence list.

There were a lot of guns. Bolt-actions. Semi-automatics. Shotguns. Pistols. Gradually, the shopping cart became so full that we had to put the long guns on end, with the barrels sticking up, so the cart looked like some sort of mechanical porcupine. There must have been thirty different rifles and half as many handguns.

At last, they told us to sign for the guns and said we could leave. I said, "Fine, which way do we go?"

"Same way you came up. Just take the elevator."

I'm thinking, this is some sort of trap, something to catch me now, since they couldn't nail Dean-Paul. All the same, I wanted to get out of there in a very bad way, so we wheeled the shopping cart full of guns into the elevator and pushed the "Lobby" button.

About two floors down, the car stopped and the doors opened for a couple to get on. They took a step toward the elevator car, and then noticed us and our shopping cart full of guns. I can only imagine what was running through their minds. They

---

Opposite: Working on our disguises for our future crime spree. Dean-Paul and I, about 1954, near the pool at 601.

paused, grinned faintly, and retreated, saying, "Oh, we'll wait for the next car down."

When the car reached the lobby, I expected the doors to open to reveal an entire SWAT team drawing a bead on us, alerted by the couple upstairs. Instead, we wheeled the cart of guns out into the lobby of the bank, and I began pushing it past the entire row of tellers' cages, each with a little line of customers.

Almost instantly, the chatter faded and I felt every eye turning to look at us. The only sound was the squeaking of the shopping cart and the metallic clinking of the gun barrels bumping against each other as we made our way to the main door. If this was some sort of a set-up, now is when it was coming down.

Nothing. Not a word. Chuck held the door open for Mom, and then for me to wheel the cart out onto the sidewalk, over to the car, and I transferred all the guns into the big trunk of the Rolls. The irony of the whole moment struck me, and I felt the prosecution of Dean-Paul had been ludicrous.

We were gun nuts, but we weren't gun-runners. We always had a healthy respect for firearms and appreciated the craftsmanship that went into an automatic weapon. Guns were a hobby, not a means for criminal gain. If we had been collecting guns to lead a life of crime, I certainly had my chance that day in the bank. The Bonnie and Clyde gang riding off in a Rolls would have been my style, if not Mom's.

Dean-Paul never owned another gun, which I'm sure was difficult for him. He understood he had played too loose with the federal regulations regarding selling automatic weapons and, as a felon, he could never possess a firearm again. Many years later, however, he joined the Air Force and became a pilot. Although Dean-Paul couldn't legally own a .22 caliber pistol, Uncle Sam deemed him fit to fly a multimillion-dollar fighter jet, outfitted with missiles, bombs, and Gatling guns.

Just another one of those gun-control loopholes, I guess.

chapter 5

The Famous Father

I remember being about 8 years old, up in my bedroom at 601 Mountain, when Mom came in and said, "Ricci, I want you to come downstairs and meet someone."

It was Marilyn Monroe. Even at that young age, I had heard of her. But I didn't realize what a legend she was or would become: the most famous international sex symbol of the twentieth century. I just thought she was some pretty woman who was in the movies with Dad. Granted, I had yet to go through puberty. For now, my frame of reference was that she was some nice lady Dad knew from work.

That all changed when I walked into the living room. Marilyn was sitting at the bar, a cigarette in her hand and a drink on the counter. For the first time in my life, I was aware of the feeling that this was somebody unique, a person who had a distinctive presence that radiated through the room. It wasn't electricity, but it was something that you could absolutely feel, even for me at that young age. I remember her turning around as Mom introduced me, and how she said in that breathless, husky voice, "Hi, Ricci."

I always cherished that brief encounter. My brother Dean-Paul even had a date with Marilyn, although he was about 11 years old at the time. We had received six season tickets from the Dodgers because of Dad's regular appearances in the charity

The pretty lady who worked with Dad. Jerry, Marilyn Monroe, Dad, Milton Berle, Averell Harriman.

celebrity baseball game with the team each year. They were incredible seats, right at field level along the first base line between home plate and the Dodger dugout, and our family went to the games frequently in those days. When Mom offered Marilyn the tickets, she wanted to take Dean-Paul along with her and Wally Cox, the venerable character actor of movies and TV who starred in the *Mr. Peepers* series and later was a regular on the quiz show *Hollywood Squares*.

On the day of the game, a black limousine with Marilyn and Wally pulled in front of our house, and Mom took Dean-Paul out to the car. As the back door of the limo opened, a cloud of smoke came wafting out, pungent with the smell of marijuana. Dean-Paul climbed in and off they went. He had a great time at the game with Marilyn, although he always had a little difficulty remembering the details.

I thought about Dean-Paul's date with Marilyn decades later, when my wife, Annie, and I were invited by our dear friends Pam and Mark Fischer to join them at a Dodger's game, using tickets they had bought at a fundraiser donated by baseball great Steve Garvey, another L.A. escapee living near us in Utah. Walking into the stadium with the Fischers and Steve and his wife, Candace, brought back many good memories, and just a twinge of regret that I hadn't been old enough to join Dean-Paul at that game so long ago with Marilyn Monroe.

She was beautiful, of course, but there was sadness to her beauty. I met Marilyn when she was having a tough time in her life, which would end tragically a short time later. She and Dad were making a movie in the summer of 1962 called *Something's Got to Give*, and it was not going well; indeed, everything was about to give. Marilyn had been showing up late or missing work completely on the movie set, flying off to John F. Kennedy's birthday party in Madison Square Garden, disappearing for days at a time, and creating major headaches for the studio. Marilyn had a saying that she always lived up to: "I've been on a calendar, but never on time."

Dad had agreed to do the movie because Marilyn had specifically asked him to co-star. Dad had known her for several years, before she had ever dated Frank or Joe DiMaggio, and he was a lot like a father figure to her, as were most of the men in her life. He was supportive and patient, even though I'm sure he was getting frustrated over the repeated delays. Finally, the executives at 20th Century Fox had enough. They sued Marilyn for failing to meet her contractual obligations for the production and announced she was going to be replaced in the movie with Lee Remick. Dad felt the studio was being too heavy handed in firing

Marilyn, and he said, "If she's not doing this picture, I'm not doing this picture." He had nothing against Lee Remick, but he wanted to stand by Marilyn.

Then the studio sued Dad as well, charging him with breach of contract and demanding $3 million in damages. Things got very messy. Dad, through his own production company, filed a countersuit for nearly $7 million against the studio, claiming that his reputation was being smeared by the Fox executives, who were trying to blacklist him from other picture deals.

Dad talked to Marilyn off and on, as things got more intense with the studio trying to exert its power over two of Hollywood's biggest box office draws. All of a sudden one morning, the family packed up and drove to the Alisal Ranch, a dude ranch in the Santa Ynez Valley near Santa Barbara.

It was an unusual trip because everyone went—Mom, Dad, all us kids, and our grandmother Peggy. We didn't usually take family vacations, just a few holiday weekends in the desert or a trip to Las Vegas while Dad performed. This was different because Dad was along and he wasn't working. I never thought of it at the time, but in a way, the Martin family decided to just disappear for a while. Only a few people knew where we were.

The Alisal had a reputation as a low-key Hollywood getaway; Clark Gable got married in the ranch-house library in the 1940s. It only hosted about thirty guests at a time and offered things like hayrides, calf-roping lessons, and trail rides on saddle horses. There were little cabins for everyone, and I remember marveling at the little instant coffee makers that automatically turned on from the weight of water poured into the glass carafe. There was a big ranch house where all the guests had their meals, and all sorts of cowboy gear was displayed on the walls. It was like we were playing on the set of one of Dad's western movies.

The Alisal was primitive, but it must have had a telephone because I remember Mom and Dad getting the phone call while we were there. They gathered us together, which was quite a feat

Myself, Dad, and Dean-Paul at the annual celebrity-pro charity baseball game at Dodger Stadium.

because we were a big troop and all doing things at opposite ends of the back forty.

"We've got to go back home now," Mom said. "Marilyn died."

We all knew whom she meant. It was one of those moments that you remember where you were, and how time seemed to stand still. Even at that age, almost 9 years old, I knew that this was bad. As much as we may have wanted one more hayride, we did not protest.

While Marilyn Monroe seemed to flash through our family life like a falling star, other actresses paid regular visits to our house and became part of the extended Martin family. Dad was a ladies man in the sense that women liked being around him, and Mom never seemed to mind that at all. One of my friend Billy Hinsche's most vivid memories is coming over to our house and seeing this stunning woman in the backyard, admiring flowers. It was Doris Day, who had just stopped by to visit.

One time, Mom brought Stella Stevens home for Dad to meet. She had met Stella somewhere and they hit it off well, and Stella said how much she loved Dean, so Mom said, "Well, why

Fatally beautiful. Marilyn with Dad at the Sands.

don't you say hello?" You'd think one of the last things a wife would want to do is bring home a bombshell to hubby, but there was Mom, a dose of va-va-va-voom in tow. Stella went on to star with Dad in one of the Matt Helm movies.

Mom did the same thing later with Ursula Andress, bringing her home to meet Dad. Ursula became a frequent guest at our parties and our ranch house in Thousand Oaks and was always a gracious, warm person. Easy on the eyes, too.

Many years later, I had to laugh when the FBI released to the public some of the contents of the confidential file they kept on Dad during the era of J. Edgar Hoover, who always had his G-men snooping into the private lives of celebrities. The file included notations of information received by the FBI in November 1955 from "an admitted homosexual" who told the feds that "he had heard Dean Martin [was] classified as 'gay.'"

News to me, and I'm sure it would be to Dad. Leave it to the FBI.

Dad was no slouch when it came to appreciating gorgeous women. I remember him telling me about shooting the movie *Bandolero!* with Raquel Welch and Jimmy Stewart. In Dad's last scene, his outlaw character, Dee, was mortally wounded and dying. The scene called for Raquel to kneel down and hold Dad's head as Jimmy, who played Dad's brother, delivered a fairly long piece of dialogue. Dad's head was to be cradled against Raquel's ample bosom, which is perhaps every dying man's last wish. Before they began shooting the scene, Dad went up to Jimmy and asked him to flub his lines several times, so they would have to keep shooting the scene over again. That would make more time for Dad in the valley of the shadow of breast. Dad reasoned that with Jimmy's trademark stutter, no one would catch on that they were in cahoots.

So the shooting began, Dad went down for the count, and Raquel nuzzled his head to her chest. Jimmy began his lines, the first of three pages of dialogue in the script. And he delivered every word flawlessly. One take, that's a wrap, great job folks. Jimmy just grinned at Dad, who never forgave him for "welching" on that deal.

Becoming friends with the great stars of Hollywood wasn't the only result of Dad's celebrity status. As we were ricocheting bullets off basement walls and trying not to blow up the gardener, Dad was about to shake up our world in a way none of us had ever expected. With the advent of his television show in September 1965, I would come to realize just how many millions of people recognized my father.

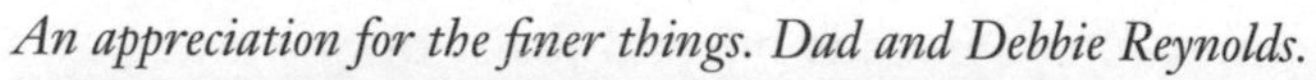

An appreciation for the finer things. Dad and Debbie Reynolds.

I knew Dad did not want to do a TV show. He was comfortable in his routine, working six weeks in Vegas twice a year, doing a movie now and then, recording an album when he found some songs he liked, all in the measured pace that allowed him to golf in the mornings and make it home for dinner in the evenings. Weekends were spent around the pool and in the living room at the house, playing with us kids.

It was a predictable pattern for a working man with a big family. Dad did not want to take on another job for fear he would lose more of this private time that he cherished more than anything. Plus, he had seen other stars venture into the new medium and find themselves trapped, unable to return to movies or the stage.

So when NBC approached him with a pitch to turn his earlier color specials into a weekly TV variety series, he really didn't want to do it. He finally agreed to host a show for just a year, as long as he only had to work one day a week. In return NBC paid him about $40,000 a show, or about $5,000 an hour.

Although the first season was a success, Dad was still not interested in continuing the show and looked forward to going back to his routine. When NBC came calling with a multiyear contract for *The Dean Martin Show*, Dad figured he would squelch the idea by making outrageous demands beyond just working one day a week. He asked for a ton of money in addition to the unheard-of rule of just one rehearsal, expecting NBC would say, "Forget it."

Instead, the network agreed to Dad's light, one-day-a-week work schedule and his hefty paycheck, paying him nearly $300,000 a show plus stock in NBC's parent company, RCA. It was the biggest contract for any TV star at the time. At a news conference on the deal, a reporter asked him how he could do the

---

Opposite: Dean-Paul helping Dad practice for the charity baseball games, in our backyard at 601 Mountain, 1958. (Allan Grant photo)

show and still drink so much. Dad's answer: "Do you think NBC would spend that much money on a drunk?"

The gamble paid off for NBC. Dad's show tied *Family Affair* on CBS for the fourteenth highest rated show in the 1966–67 season, then climbed to number eight in the Nielsen ratings the following two seasons, dropping back to fourteen by 1970. Dad won the Golden Globe in 1967 for Best Male TV Star and was nominated for the same award again in 1968 and 1969, and for Best TV Actor in a Musical/Comedy in the 1970 Golden Globe nominations.

Over its nine-year, prime-time run, Dad's Thursday night show, and its various off-season replacements such as *Dean Martin Presents the Golddiggers* and *The Dean Martin Summer Show*, was responsible more than any other aspect of his career for creating millions of fans who still appreciate him today.

For me, television was the medium that changed everything. Suddenly, Dad was in everyone's living room each week, and millions of people were sitting down watching him: mothers, fathers, and kids. It was different from the movies and the records and the stage shows that Dad had done. Kids my age wouldn't normally have access to those arenas of his career. Las Vegas shows were generally off-limits to kids, as were a lot of the movies Dad made—the genre known as "bedroom comedies."

Television changed that, and kids at school started talking about this guy on TV—that's Ricci's dad. Later, as they grew older, the kids who watched him on television started going to Dad's movies, especially the Matt Helm films that hit during the secret agent craze of James Bond spy movies and TV shows like *The Man from U.N.C.L.E.* and *Mission: Impossible*.

I was about 12 years old when Dad's show took off, and instantly I noticed people started changing around me at school, treating me differently, a little more special than before. All the same, I don't remember looking at Dad any differently than I had growing up. He was still the same guy who came home through

Ain't that a kick in the head. Dad giving it to the bad guys in a scene from The Silencers, *1965. Of course, we had to try this at home.*

the back hallway, into the kitchen, buttering that slice of bread and moseying by with a little pinch on my neck and the standard, "Whaddya say, pallie?"

TV was a much stronger force in pop culture back then than today. Dad's show was a smash in an era of nationalized television, when the big three networks were all that was on. Television sets had knobs that clicked to thirteen channels and UHF. Less than half of those positions had network programs on them. There were no cable and no satellite services providing hundreds of alternatives in television programming. A hit network TV show was something the entire country was familiar with.

With his rugged good looks, a voice as natural as singing in the shower, a penchant for one-liners, and that regular-guy nonchalance, Dad not only charmed the women viewers but played well with men, who saw Dino as the kind of guy they could sit down with and have a drink and a laugh. The set of the show, with its cozy bar and den, seemed to invite viewers to kick back with a cocktail and enjoy a little crooning, teasing, and laughter. That mainstream appeal allowed Dad to get away with things on the show that, done by anyone else, would not have been met with laughs. Whether it was his I-got-a-good-buzz-on routine or walking onstage with one of the Golddigger girls on a leash, people knew Dad meant no offense. He just loved a good joke.

Because of Dad's unwavering requirement that he only do one walk-through rehearsal before the show was filmed in front of a studio audience, his ad-libs, flubs, and freewheeling style became the biggest attraction of the series. Although some of his guests never could get used to rehearsing all week without the star, neither the show nor Dad seemed to suffer as a result. As far as the musical aspect of the show's format, Dad needed very little rehearsing. He had it upstairs.

You would never hear him singing or humming around the house. He was not the kind to pace the living room floor with a script, practicing his lines out loud. Like the saying goes, he left his work at the office. His routine for rehearsing for the TV show, which usually was filmed Sunday evenings at an NBC soundstage in Burbank, was to listen to a cassette of the songs scheduled for the upcoming show that producers would make for him the week before. He would listen to the music in his car on his way to golf and on the drive home, singing to himself. Most of the songs were ones Dad knew anyway.

He always went into the skits on the show cold, reading directly from the cue cards that the stagehands would hold up as the cameras rolled. It became part of an atmosphere of not-putting-on-airs that was Dad's trademark, lousing up his lines on purpose (or just as often for real), joking about his eyesight, boozing it up. That bit would transform the driest comedy skit into a hilarious shambles, leaving the audience in the studio and at home creasing up with laughter.

The unpredictability set Dad's show apart from other contemporary variety programs like *The Lawrence Welk Show* and *The*

Opposite: A drink, a joke, and no rehearsals.

Ed Sullivan Show, with their stiff hosts, long hemlines, and tight formulas. It became a ritual on Thursday nights for millions of families to sit down and watch to see how Dad would ad-lib his way out of this one.

Our family was the same as the rest of America, gathering each week in our living room to watch Dad on his show, even though it aired at 10 P.M. on the West Coast, late for a school night. We seldom went to the filming of the show, although my oldest brother, Craig, was hired by Dad's producer, Greg Garrison, as a production assistant and later as associate producer.

Greg hired me when I was 16 to shoot still photographs of the show each week, using the pictures for his production company as publicity shots. My job was to quietly stand next to the camera crane, taking photographs of the various skits, choruses, and duets during the show.

When the show broke for a set change, I would follow Dad back down a hallway to his little dressing room, closest to the set, where he would either get into costume for a skit or song, or sit on the couch with the TV on while Greg discussed the next segment or the cue card guy brought in his lines to review.

"OK, pallie," Dad would say to the cue card man, who would then hold the cards up for Dad to see. Dad would read out loud once, getting into the rhythm of the lines, maybe asking a couple of questions. This was pretty much a full rehearsal for him.

Dad would dress himself and do his own hair for the show, with the makeup girl stepping in to quickly touch up his face for the next segment. Periodically, a guest would poke their head in the door—Greg had strict orders that no one was allowed to go in and pal around with Dad.

It was a fun experience for me, watching various regulars like Charles Nelson Reilly, Dom Deluise, and Ruth Buzzi do a quick, open-and-shut "Hi, Dean, howya doin'?" greeting at Dad's door during the shows. It was good etiquette to thank the host for having you on the show, but with Dad's absence during the weekday

Bing Crosby, Dad, and Phil Harris winging it during Dad's 1958 color TV special, "The Dean Martin Show," which would eventually lead to his weekly NBC show. (Allan Grant photo)

rehearsals and Greg's strict rules on fraternizing with Dad, celebrities knew it had to be a quickie if they wanted to speak to him offstage.

My older sister Gail became a regular, singing on Dad's show beginning with a summer special in 1967 and then on the fall schedule in 1968. Fans loved her duets with Dad. She had taken voice lessons while in college, and after Dad heard her singing at home in her room, she started singing at a few nightclubs with a repertoire Dad and Frank Sinatra suggested. Later, Deana and Dean-Paul also made guest appearances with Dad, always to positive fan response.

Dad would have Mom and all of us kids on the show for a few Christmas specials, usually singing a song with the Sinatra children. Those Christmas shows were the only times Mom went to the studio because, as we all found out after a day's rehearsal, the making of a variety show is not as glamorous as the final version appears on television.

Like movies under production, the creation of a television show is basically boring. I found this out right away when I started

Jiving with the kings. Sammy, Frank, George Burns, Dad, Jack Benny, and Milton Berle at a SHARE benefit show.

taking pictures on the set for Greg. There are hours of lighting, blocking, and run-throughs that the viewer never sees. No wonder Dad refused rehearsals. It would have been the death of the casual ease and naturalness that was the show's biggest draw.

At home, Dad's increased fame had no impact inside the house, but it became a windfall for us out on the street. There was a steady procession of tourists and fans driving by 601 Mountain, hoping for any glimpse of Dad or the Dean Martin family, and we were happy to accommodate the burgeoning interest. Dad would even practice his chip shot on a section of the lawn in front of the Mountain Drive entrance, sometimes chatting and taking pictures with the tourists.

To raise fast cash, Gina and I would raid the supply closet upstairs and set up a drive-by souvenir shop of toothpaste, toothbrushes, bar soap, and other household supplies. When the tourists came by, we'd sell them our supply-closet items so they could say they had a bar of soap from Dean Martin's house. It was a booming business, especially on Sundays, when people parked their cars at the end of the driveway to take pictures of the house. Huge tour buses—which were prohibited from stopping—would slowly cruise by, one every 15 minutes on weekends.

Even today, tour buses still pull up in front of Mom's house in Palm Springs, the little vacation cottage that she and Dad bought back in 1954. On occasions when we're visiting Mom there, my three young daughters—Pepper Jazz, Montana Sage, and Rio-Dean—carry on the Martin kids' tradition by setting up a lemonade stand for the tourists. So far, Mom has not reported any missing toothbrushes after the bus leaves.

At 601, we took to playing pranks on the fans who would pull up in front of the house to get a glimpse of the Martins. Jay Judson, our best friend from the neighborhood, was a stocky guy, just like many of the tourists. When Jay was old enough to drive, we hatched a plan over the phone to have Jay drive up to our house acting like a tourist. I would tease and make fun of him, and then walk back toward the house while he crept up behind me with a large rock, intending to bean me. We wanted to see if the tourists outside would stop him.

On cue, Jay drove up to the house and began taking pictures while standing beside two heavy-set women who were also taking snapshots of 601. I came out of the house, saw Jay, and started yelling. "Hey, fat boy! Get out of here! Get off our property, tubby!" Jay fired back and we exchanged more insults as I told him to scram. Then I turned and walked toward the back door and Jay came up behind me, picking up one of the big stones that bordered the driveway.

By now, the two ladies were mesmerized by this seeming homicide in the making. Jay came up behind me and raised the rock over his head as I pretended not to notice. We both expected a scream any second, warning me to watch out. But the two tourists just stood and watched. I guess they figured I had it coming.

Improvising, Jay slammed the rock down beside me, pretending to miss. We tussled on the ground, then I ran into the house and he followed me inside, where we both yelled and bumped around, hoping the audience outside could hear. There was a crate of empty milk bottles near the back door, where the milk delivery man would pick them up. As our fake fight finale, I pretended to throw Jay out of the house and tossed a couple of milk bottles onto the carport for effect.

What the tourists saw was Jay being bounced out of the house amid a shower of broken glass. Jay ran to his car, yelling at me over his shoulder, and drove off. The two tourists never flinched or said a word as the commotion unfolded. After a few minutes, I guess they realized things had quieted down and they left. Just another day at the Dean Martin home, they figured.

Fame was such a standard part of growing up that I don't think any of us kids really recognized that this kind of attention was that unusual. It was the same for many of our friends and neighbors.

For example, I remember watching Desi Arnaz Jr., the son of Lucille Ball and Desi Arnaz, play the drums in one of our classrooms at Beverly Hills Catholic School, when we were both in grade school. The nuns had asked anyone with musical talent to demonstrate it at school, sort of a show-and-tell exercise. Desi had brought his drum kit to school and performed in each classroom during the day. The students and nuns clapped, and my brother Dean-Paul approached him about joining a rock and roll band he was putting together, a group that became Dino, Desi, and Billy.

Desi remains one of my dearest friends. We took the stage together at the MGM Grand in Las Vegas in November 1999 for a salute to Dino, Desi, and Billy, dubbed "Ricci, Desi, and Billy," performing some of their hits from the 1960s as the opening act for Al Jardine's Beach Boys Family and Friends. It was a great treat for me to be playing the MGM Grand, where Dad had head-

Dean-Paul, age 3, and myself, age 1, with Mom at 601 Mountain in 1954.

lined a dozen years earlier. As Dad felt about the Rat Pack performances, it's more fun working with good friends on stage than just being solo. They take a verse, you take a verse, it's not just you, you, you.

I never looked at Desi as the son of famous parents, just as I was not really aware that other kids in the neighborhood and at school were the progeny of celebrities. Besides Desi, there were Miguel and Maria Ferrer, the children of actor José Ferrer and singer Rosemary Clooney; Patricia Martin, the daughter of Broadway actress Mary Martin; Steve Carey, son of the veteran movie and TV actor Macdonald Carey; and Hunt and Tony Sales, the sons of actor Soupy Sales. It seemed perfectly normal.

I don't remember even acknowledging that they or their parents were somehow important because they made movies or were entertainers. That was what my Dad did, so it seemed natural that the other kids I played with had parents whose jobs were similar to my father's. We had nothing else to compare it to.

That's not to say there weren't a few blips on my radar screen that something was a bit odd. I remember being only about 7 or 8 years old, taking a bath in a tub that was frothy with Mr. Bubble. My grandmother was keeping an eye on me as I played with my boats, and she had shampooed my hair into a bubbly, pointy turban. I'm sure I looked like a character from a Dr. Seuss book. When Mom came into the bathroom to check on me, she saw my goofy hair and decided it would be cute to show some friends downstairs at a party she was having. She asked my grandmother to carry me down to the stairway landing just outside the living room.

There I was, wrapped in a towel and my hair in a foamy pinnacle, when a tan, huge, unbelievably striking man walked in the front door on his way to the party in the living room. Ahead of me on the steps, Mom waved him over saying, "Stewart, I want you to meet my son, Ricci." The legendary actor Stewart Granger looked up at me, broke into a grin of impossibly white teeth, and roared with laughter, prompting other guests to look over and join in.

Going back up the stairs to my now lukewarm bath, I remember thinking, "What was that all about?"

At school, Dad's stardom from the TV show perhaps prompted me to polish my own image. Leaving Beverly Hills Catholic School and its uniforms following the fifth grade, I transferred to Hawthorne, a big public school, and began to perfect my own look. A turtleneck sweater with a scarf around the neck became my preppy signature, with "A-1 Peggers" corduroy pants. An alternative to the turtleneck was a polo shirt from Rudnicks, with the collar turned up just like Dad.

I was skinny and of average height, with braces. My hair was just starting to get long in the back due to the Beatles, which in the mid-1960s was the source of much irritation for the older generation.

Hawthorne was an intimidating school, much bigger and less structured than Beverly Hills Catholic School, and it scared me to death. Dean-Paul had left Beverly Hills Catholic for Loyola, another Catholic school. All of us kids were raised Catholic, baptized, and confirmed. For some of us, it took hold. Dean-Paul was a dedicated altar boy, competing with his friends to see who could do the most masses and keeping track in a little booklet. I, on the other hand, was not as full of the spirit. During confirmation, when we were asked to stand up to take a vow of abstinence, swearing off caffeine, tobacco, and other vices, I remained seated. I knew even then that I wanted to keep my options open.

So, while Dean-Paul chose the Jesuits at Loyola, I opted for the masses at Hawthorne. I quickly came to regret the choice, overwhelmed by the size of the student body and the impersonal nature of a big public school. One afternoon in shop class, while I was hunched over some birdhouse project, the principal of the school came up behind me, grabbed the back of my hair, gave it a tug, and said, "You don't need all that hair, do ya, Martin?" I was mortified. At home, I told Mom what had happened and she said, "That's it, you're out of there."

Thus began an odyssey in search of another school, a lengthy process of visiting various private schools and interviewing with faculty members about how I might do under their tutelage. They all were stuffy and snobby, and Mom and I would leave each interview with bad vibes.

Finally, Mom found a school called Rexford, and we went to meet with the principal and his wife, the vice principal. We sat down in their office, and both of them immediately lit up cigarettes. Mom turned to me and said, "This is the school for you."

Rexford was a small private school, just three kids per classroom, in a drab building next to a dry cleaners at Rexford Street and Olympic Boulevard. The school was intended to help students who were slow learners, but we always wondered if those impediments might be improved a bit if the classrooms weren't always fragrant with the chemical fumes of the "One-Hour Martinizing" shop next door.

The school had no P.E. class, no sports teams, and no music program. The grounds were basically the size of a small yard, with a couple of benches and no playground equipment. Lunch was served not in a cafeteria, but from the back of one of those catering trucks that you see at construction sites. The truck had no grill for preparing meals. Instead, it had a warmer for burrito dogs—a hot dog wrapped in a tortilla—and a tray of ice and drinks.

Rexford was about as bare bones and unpretentious as you could get, and from the time I started in sixth grade, I loved it. The laid-back nature of the faculty, the small student body, and the absence of cliquish clubs created a learning environment that was tailor-made for kids weary of the prep-school routine. It seemed less like school and more like hanging out with friends. For skeptical parents, Rexford was able to allay any concerns about a lack of discipline by producing students with good grades.

My scholastic success in the casual atmosphere of Rexford prompted Dean-Paul to leave Loyola—where he was having his own battles over hair length—and switch to Rexford. Deana would follow.

Word got out about this new school the Martin kids were going to, and the Sinatras sent their daughter Tina to Rexford. Tina Sinatra was Deana's age, born in 1948, three years older than my brother Dean-Paul. Like his fellow band member Desi Arnaz Jr., Dean-Paul was madly in love with Tina. He and Desi even wrote a song about her, "She Doesn't See Me," which accurately described her interest in them. Tina was a little aloof when it came to the romantic overtures of Dean-Paul and Desi.

Other children of celebrities or celebrity kids followed our migration to Rexford—Henry Mancini's two daughters, Monica and Felice, and Jon Provost, who played Timmy in the TV show *Lassie* from 1957 to 1964. We created a ragtag pack, and eventually the class size grew to twelve students per teacher. The learning pace was slow and discipline was lax, so we took full advantage of the situation. It wasn't unusual to see kids smoking in the yard with the teachers during break.

I eventually got the award for longest attendance, graduating from Rexford after six years from grades 7 through 12. I pretty much owned the place by my senior year, and I would take my physical science teacher, Jim Baker, to lunch at the Luau restaurant in Beverly Hills, where we would have martinis. A casual visitor to Rexford would find it hard to tell the difference between the inmates and the guards.

What it lacked in regimen, Rexford made up in results. The pace and style of the teaching was effective, and the informality in the classroom fostered understanding of issues that could never be gleaned from a textbook. One of those moments for me came during a ninth-grade social studies class.

It was 1968 and Martin Luther King Jr. had been assassinated. The class was discussing civil rights, racial inequity, and desegregation. Trying to illustrate that most of the students weren't exposed to racial diversity in their daily lives, the teacher, Herb Richardson, said, "With the exception of Ricci, you all would probably feel uncomfortable at a party that was strictly black."

The statement struck me, not so much because he had singled me out, but because he had recognized something in my behavior and demeanor that had never occurred to me. There was no pretense about color in my eyes, because a racial barrier had never been presented to me growing up. I was taken aback with the realization, however naively, that the color of a person's skin was a reason for some people to dislike others.

As I got older, I was shocked to see prejudice and bigotry. I had come from an environment where there had never been a question of race. I had grown up with a black family who lived with us at 601 Mountain from my earliest memories. Freddie and Alma Johnson, and their daughter Sandra, were a part of our family, with Freddie driving us around and running errands, while Alma cooked and did some cleaning. They had a small living room and bedrooms on the main floor of the house, and we would eat together, play together, and joke around together, absent of any distinction of class or race.

In the second grade, I remember breaking down and sobbing at school the day Freddie died. The nuns had to call Mom to come and get me because I was inconsolable. Dad and Mom reassured Alma that she would always have a place in our home as a member of our family, and they made sure that Sandra's schooling and living needs were taken care of. Dad went to Freddie's funeral in Watts to show how much he cared for and respected Freddie.

Alma worked and lived with us for twenty-five years and was fiercely protective of Dad and our family. I remember how my best friend from high school, Wayne Tweed, would come to the house to visit by going to the back door and knocking. Wayne, who has remained my closest friend to this day, would later tell

Dean-Paul's third birthday party at 601 Mountain, 1954.

me that he came to recognize that if Alma "didn't like you, you would know right away. She kept an eye on anybody who came to the house because this was their home, too. There was a powerful sense of loyalty there."

One day, Wayne came over and, as usual, knocked on the back door. Alma said, with a little impatience, "Wayne, you don't have to knock. Just come on in." Wayne later told me, "Long before I had realized it, she had accepted me and expected me to feel free to walk in as if it was my own home. My constant knocking had become a pain."

Wayne was three years ahead of me at Rexford, the most popular guy in school, towering six-foot-three over my five-foot frame. I'm sure we made quite the odd couple, a tall black guy hanging out with a "scrawny"—Wayne's word—white kid. We were drawn together by shared interests: we both loved motorcycles, guns, and trucks.

In time, we became inseparable. Wayne would come over to our house after school, joining Dean-Paul and me in our adventures in detonation and dirt-biking. I would spend every weekend at Wayne's house, which was across the basin to the south in a nice neighborhood known as View Park, the area where Ray Charles lived. Wayne's father, Dr. Andre Tweed, was the first black board-certified forensic psychiatrist in the state of California, and in many ways he was like Dad. Not a lot of words, but when he did say something, it was a zinger. He also made the best waffles—or "war-fulls," as Dr. Tweed would say—I've ever tasted.

Those weekend sleepovers at Wayne's were a first for me, since I had never had much cause to leave my sanctuary at 601. In retrospect, Wayne and I have marveled at how easygoing our parents were with our friendship. At a time when racial hatred and tension was perhaps at its zenith in America, our friendship seemed perfectly natural. We never thought of ourselves as black and white, just two pallies interested in making stuff go faster or explode louder.

Wayne still remembers the first time he met Dad. We were hanging out in the projection room, shooting some pool, and snacking on a big bowl of Bugles, the little cone-shaped snack crackers that Mom always kept in supply.

"I'm standing there by the pool table and in comes this giant of a man, walking slow and easy, like he was conserving energy," Wayne said. "He's in his khakis and cashmere sweater, wearing these velvet slippers with the embroidered crest and crown on them, and he comes up to me and says, 'You must be Wayne-oh, pallie.' And I'm trembling. 'Uh, hi, Mr. Martin.' And he stuck out his huge hand and shook mine, just naturally gracious and making me feel from that point on as comfortable as I ever was in another person's home."

Even after the Frank Sinatra Jr. kidnapping scare, when three men snatched Frank's nineteen-year-old son in 1963 from a Lake Tahoe casino and then returned him after collecting $240,000 in ransom, my parents never hesitated to let me spend time at Wayne's house. They knew and loved Wayne, and they knew that he was a product of caring parents. Wayne later told me that one day he answered the phone at home and a voice on the other end asked, "Could I speak to Mrs. Tweed please?"

Wayne asked, "Who's calling please?"

The voice said, "It's Dean Martin."

A bit surprised, Wayne handed the phone to his mother, Ruth, who was stunned. Dad had called just to thank her for taking care of his boy Rico and for having me over to the house so often, and to tell her Wayne was always welcome at our home. Wayne said that call meant a lot to his mother and father, coming from Dad when he was at the height of his fame.

When I heard about the call, I was pretty impressed myself, since Dad never phoned anyone and he usually stayed out of his children's socializing. Our families never got together, although there was always an open invitation to Dr. and Mrs. Tweed to come to one of Mom's parties. While they demurred, Wayne became a regular fixture at those events. He tells the story about going into the powder room at one party at 601 and heading for the door to the toilet. Just as he reached for the doorknob, the door swung open and Angie Dickinson emerged.

Another time, Wayne met Don Rickles in the foyer—alone. Don was one of the few guests at the parties at 601 who made us all a little nervous. He was a sawed-off shotgun of a man, someone who would get up in the morning, brush his teeth, and sharpen his tongue. Don was hugely popular, doing what he did best, which was ridicule people without mercy. He used to hammer Dad, doubling over everyone with laughter. But you never wanted to be on the receiving end when Rickles pulled the trigger.

Wayne was coming under the big staircase on his way to the front door when he encountered Don Rickles coming out of the living room, locked and loaded, just itching to fire. "I was certain he was going to let go on me, and I was scared because I had seen him nail Sammy Davis Jr. to the parquet floor with his verbal blasts," said Wayne. "But he looked at me and paused, then just nodded and walked right by. I can't tell you what a relief that was. I think he knew I was embraced by this family, and his look said, 'I'll let this one go.'"

Wayne was comfortable around our house, and we would hang out with some of Dad's friends who sometimes came over when their golf game was rained out, guys like Richard Dawson, Tony Bennett, and Dick Martin of *Laugh-In*. Wayne's ultimate initiation came during one of those afternoons, while he was walking out of the living room and Dad was coming in. As they passed, Dad hauled off and gave Wayne a stinger punch just below his right shoulder, prompting Wayne to do an exaggerated pratfall, sprawling animatedly onto the floor. Dad grinned: "Not bad for 51 years old, hey pallie?"

"I knew he loved me at that point," Wayne said. "He wouldn't give a shot like that to anyone but his friends. I had heard he was a boxer as a kid and I can tell you he still had it. I remember

Never a dull moment. Michael Romanoff (seated, left) with Mom and Dad on the party circuit.

going to his birthday party twenty years later at the private room at Mateo's and reminding him of that punch, and he was surprised I remembered it."

Wayne came along on a family vacation we took aboard John Wayne's private motor yacht, the *Wild Goose*. The boat began life as a military mine sweeper and had luxurious quarters, an attentive crew, and a galley that produced incredible meals. We spent three days cruising the California coast and were met at the dock when we returned by the Duke himself.

Dad's affection for my friend Wayne was such that he granted a rare interview to him one afternoon, when we were goofing around with one of the first black-and-white videotape recorders. I ran the camera and Wayne did his best Walter Cronkite, asking Dad all sorts of questions about life, love, and fame. Mom even popped in and gleefully monitored the interrogation, which Dad relished. It was a given among reporters in Hollywood that Dean Martin rarely consented to interviews.

Instead, his agent or publicity people would do the interviews, telling the reporter to just quote them as Dad.

One day, when Wayne and I were driving to a rehearsal of a band we had formed called Soul Support, my obliviousness to racial differences was burst like a bubble. Our Pontiac station wagon was loaded down with gear. As we approached an intersection, Wayne didn't see a car that had the right-of-way and started to pull out. The other car honked and Wayne stopped short, but as the guy in the other car drove by, he screamed curses and the infamous "n-word" at Wayne.

Wayne was furious. I had never seen him so angry. I tried to calm him down, but he was outraged that this guy would yell such an ugly word at him for an honest mistake. For the first time, I recognized that the color of Wayne's skin was a flashpoint for some whites, something to ridicule and look down upon. I saw how hurtful that was to Wayne, and I was ashamed.

Several times, Wayne went with us to Las Vegas to see Dad perform. On one of those trips, we were supposed to meet the daughter of an important South African surgeon. Someone had decided that the kids might enjoy spending the day together, so Wayne and I were to meet this young woman in the casino restaurant. We were sitting at a table, eating the dollar pancake special, when she walked up, horrified. She looked at me with disgust and said, "How can you eat breakfast with a black man?"

We got her back the next day. After I arranged to meet her alone in my room, Wayne and I ordered plates of sausages, bacon, and other breakfast items from room service, then placed the food all over the room, with sausages on the lamps, pancakes draped over the dresser, making one holy mess. We arranged pillows under the blankets to look like a body, and Wayne climbed on top of them under the blankets. When she knocked at the door, I opened it from the side and then scooted into the bathroom. As she walked into the trashed room, Wayne pretended to be doing the wild thing with his pillowy "girlfriend" under the covers.

The deputy and the sheriff. Dad and John Wayne, who starred together in one of Dad's favorite movies, Rio Bravo.

She screamed and ran out of the room as we rolled on the floor laughing.

Another time, Wayne and I drove out to the Valley with Wayne's girlfriend, Melody, to test-fire a pair of M-1 carbines we had attempted to modify into fully automatic weapons. The experiment failed, having turned the guns into single-shot rifles, requiring us to pull the slide each time we fired. Driving back home in Wayne's Jeep, I sat in the back seat while Wayne and Melody sat in front. It may have looked sort of like *Mod Squad*—black guy, white girl, white guy. And a few rifles thrown in.

A cop spotted us and pulled Wayne over—why, I'll never know. As soon as he saw the guns, he was screaming at Wayne, ordering us all out of the vehicle. Things got very tense, and there were a lot of racial overtones in the cop's actions. We wound up at Foothill Station in the holding tank. As the police checked the guns, they realized they were all legal and we had done nothing wrong. They released Wayne on his own, but since I was a minor, the secretary from the house had to come take custody of me. The whole thing was so unnecessary. But at the same time, I was glad we had failed to convert those M-1s. We would probably still be in jail.

Wayne would encounter other bigots, even at 601 Mountain. When he was 20 and trying to earn money for a trip to Europe, Mom and Dad hired him to be one of our security guards. Wayne's shift was the 9 P.M. to 5 A.M. patrol, which meant sitting in his car in the driveway. His first night, one of the local police officers pulled up in an unmarked car and walked up the drive to check out Wayne. Wayne was wearing a pistol he had bought from Dean-Paul, a Walther PPK, as a sidearm. The cop started grilling Wayne—perhaps the only black man in Beverly Hills at that time allowed to carry a gun—and the whole line of questioning made Wayne uncomfortable.

The next morning, Mom asked him how it went and he mentioned the grilling he got from the police officer. Mom was livid and said she would make sure that this officer was disciplined.

"I remember pleading with Jeanne not to make that call, because I knew that the Martin family had the pull to get things done," said Wayne. "But I asked her to let me hoe my own row and I would work it out. As upset as she was that this had happened, she let it pass. I always appreciated her for that."

After that first night, things got easier on the night patrol. Wayne was frequently joined by Officer Fred Cook, the local cop who had looked the other way when we rumbled by in our tank. Fred would park in the driveway and talk to Wayne, and on some nights, we'd gather around his squad car for pizza.

Dad periodically had a late-night craving for pizza from Miceli's, an L.A. restaurant, and he would send me to get it, treating me to a second pizza for my trouble. The folks at Miceli's were always thrilled to fill an order for Dean Martin, so they really loaded up those pizzas. While Dad ate his in front of the TV, Wayne and I sat outside with Officer Cook, drinking Coca-Cola

The lady of the house.
Mom at home at 601.

out of the little bottles and eating pizza off the warm hood of his police car.

The day Wayne left for college at Arizona State University, he came by 601 to say goodbye. I remember Mom and I standing in the driveway, hugging Wayne as he climbed into his Jeep to drive to Tempe. We realized that we would remain friends, but it also was the end of an era in both of our lives that had meant so much. We'd nurtured a genuine friendship that was void of all the racial hassles that seemed to permeate every aspect of society at the time. Now it was the end of youth's innocence.

Wayne told me years later that as he drove off, he had tears running down his cheeks. I told him that when Mom and I went inside and watched through a window that overlooked Sunset Boulevard as his Jeep drove away, she gave me a hug as we wiped away tears of our own.

chapter 6

Nice Swing

Dean Martin recorded hundreds of songs and sold millions of records. But you'd never know it around our house. If there was music playing from the phonograph, it was an album that Mom put on and we would hear artists like Dinah Washington, Peggy Lee, Lena Horne, Ella Fitzgerald, and some Johnny Mathis. You would rarely hear Frank Sinatra on our stereo. Mom thought Frank was a pain in the ass anyway, so she did not want to be reminded of him by playing one of his records.

Nor did she ever put on a Dean Martin record. That was never weird to us kids, because we just figured Dad was always singing on the radio, stage, or television, so why listen to him at home? About the only time I remember hearing Dad's records at home was during Christmas, when Mom would play his Christmas album and we'd hear songs like "Marshmallow World" and "Baby It's Cold Outside" during the holidays.

Dad never put a record on at home. He never listened to any of his records, and seldom did he listen to anyone else's records. If he had any preference at all, his favorite songs were country tunes sung by the old traditional artists. Eddie Arnold was one of his favorite singers, and you would catch a little of Eddie's influence in some of Dad's songs, numbers like "Send Me the Pillow You Dream On." Dad's preference for country

music was reflected in a couple of albums he made in 1963 under the moniker of Dean "Tex" Martin and then again late in his career with his 1983 album called "The Nashville Sessions."

His biggest singing influence, and perhaps the reason he pursued a career in entertainment, was Bing Crosby. My grandmother Angela, Dad's mother, would sometimes tell the story of Dad growing up in Steubenville and going to the movies all the time. One time, when he was still just a boy, Angela took Dad to see a Bing Crosby movie. After the movie ended, Dad turned to Angela in the theater and said, "One day, I'm going to be up there doing that. One day."

Angela always believed him. She seemed to know from his childhood that something special would happen for Dad. Pop, on the other hand, was much more practical. Guy Crocetti thought his son had better learn a trade. If Dad knew how to cut hair, he could support a family when this singing nonsense was over. Dad liked to point out in his Vegas act that most of the people he grew up with laid odds he would be neither a crooner nor a *coiffeur*, but instead end up getting the chair. And they didn't mean the barber's chair.

Because Dad idolized Bing, he grew up imitating that smooth baritone, the phrasing, and the Crosby casualness. Perhaps the only singer more casual in style was Perry Como, and when you would see Dad, Bing, and Perry singing together on Dad's TV show, it was like the Three Tenors on Quaaludes. Effortless and suave, that was Dad's style. He always thought if the singing was forced, then you weren't singing.

For all his musical grace, Dad was not a musician. He never played the piano, but once in a while he would pick up a classical guitar, the kind with the nylon strings, and strum an

---

Opposite: Singing in his sleep. The recording studio was about the only time that Dad listened to his own songs.

No hooks, no slices, just a nice smooth swing to their styles. Bing and Dad. (Eddie Carroll photo)

impromptu Spanish-style melody. He had the hands for both guitar and piano, however. They were unusually big with long fingers. "Dag, you need to get those pressed," Frank liked to joke.

One of Dad's favorite jokes, which he would pull when we went out to dinner, was to be having a conversation and absent-mindedly butter his big hands as if they were a piece of bread. He also had a standard joke of asking us for a bite of the sandwich we were eating, only to take such a huge chomp out of it that the entire middle of the sandwich was gone. We took to holding our sandwiches with both hands to stake out a boundary for the allowable bite.

Dad's big paws made him unbeatable at the game of jacks. Gina would have her ball and jacks, and Dad would sit with her on the parquet floor in the foyer at 601. She would drop the jacks so they would scatter on the floor, then bounce the ball up and scoop up the jacks in the required order, one at a time, two at a time, three at a time, while catching the ball and counting "Onesies, twosies, threesies," etc. until the last jack was recovered. It got tougher to scoop up the required number when you got into "tensies, elevensies, and twelvesies."

Dad, who had played jacks a lot as a kid—and probably bet on them—would get his turn, dropping the jacks on the ground and bouncing the ball up. In one swipe with those big hands he would collect every jack on the floor and declare himself the winner. It was one of those things he loved to do to tease us.

He did have a minor handicap in the jacks competitions, the seldom-noticed droopy pinkie on his right hand. His gimpy little finger was the result of a childhood injury, the exact cause lost to the ages. Dad told us he came into the house howling because he had knocked his pinky out of joint, and Pop, in his classic style, said to his son, "Here, I'd a fix that for you." Pop took hold of Dad's hand, gave his pinkie a quick tug, and popped the joint back into place. Dad held out his hand, and his finger was straightened, as good as new. But after a few seconds the end of the finger bent down at the last knuckle, forever off-kilter.

Those big hands certainly helped his golf game. He would rehearse not songs but swings around the house. Sitting on the couch, watching TV, Dad would have a golf club in his hand. One of my most abiding memories of him growing up was watching him practice his swing in the foyer at 601. Beyond the parquet tile, there was shag carpeting in the foyer, and Dad would stand there, crank back his swing, and unwind, just breezing the tops of the carpet fibers. He was tall—6-foot-one-inch—and on the follow-through, the head of the driver would arc within an inch of the ceiling. Dad would swing full-speed in the foyer, as if teeing off, and when we were younger, we would sit and watch him with a sense of awe that he never put a nice fat divot in Mom's sparkly white ceiling. Our attempts to emulate those practice swings were immediately interrupted by Mom's demand to take the golf club outside.

Every time is tee time. A golf club was never far from Dad's hands. (Allan Grant photo)

Dad concentrated on his golf swing intensely, but one day he really blew a drive. The story of Dad and Elvis on the golf course was told to me by Jerry Schilling, who was one of Elvis Presley's closest friends, like a brother to the King. Jerry and nine other members of Elvis's inner circle placed an eternal flame at Elvis's tombstone in Graceland. He was best friends with my future brother-in-law, Carl Wilson of the Beach Boys, who would later marry Gina.

Jerry recalled to me how Elvis idolized Dad and considered

Dad one of his biggest influences—Dad's 1955 hit "Memories Were Made of This" is a good example of their similar styles. Elvis had heard that Dad golfed regularly at the Bel-Air Country Club, so although Elvis had never golfed, he began staying in a house right on the links. One morning, Jerry and Elvis spotted Dad getting ready to tee off. Just as Dad was about to swing, Elvis waved to him, yelling "Hey, Dean! Hey, Dean, it's Elvis!"

After Dad hit the ball, he waved back at Elvis. But Jerry thought he ought to warn Elvis that interrupting someone just before they are ready to swing is bad golf etiquette. He gently explained that in the future, Elvis should probably wait until Dean was done swinging before calling to him. Elvis did not take the suggestion well, no matter how diplomatic Jerry was. Realizing his blunder, Elvis turned around and disappeared into his house. He stayed indoors for the next three days because he was so embarrassed. Jerry said he kept repeating, "I don't know about golf. I just wanted to say hi."

Many years later, I asked Dad about it, just to see what his version of the encounter was. Dad remembered that day on the course and Elvis yelling hello to him, but his take was completely different. He remarked how great it was that Elvis would say hello. Elvis's faux pas never even registered with him. He thought it was a nice thing that Elvis had done, taking a moment to wave and say hi.

Dad never really connected with the whole rock and roll era that Elvis helped usher in. It wasn't so much that he didn't like the new style of music; it was that he found the whole rock scene somewhat amusing. One time he was guest hosting a TV variety show called *The Hollywood Palace* in 1964, before he signed the NBC contract. The Rolling Stones were among the featured acts in the show, making one of their first TV appearances in America, and back then the Stones were just perfecting their hooligan look. When they finished their first song, Dad came on to take the show to a commercial break. He was grinning, almost

The swing meets The King.

laughing at the Stones. His teaser to the TV audience was something like, "Now, you all come back after this message because you wouldn't want to leave me alone with these Rolling Stones, would you?" Mick and the boys were so insulted, they stormed off the set and the second number was cancelled. Not that it hurt their careers much, however.

When it came to the Beatles, Dad would go down in history as the singer who repelled the British Invasion of American pop music. In 1964, the Beatles were dominating the Number One spot of the Billboard record charts most of the year, with songs like "I Want to Hold Your Hand," "She Loves You," "Can't Buy Me Love," and "A Hard Day's Night." On August 15, 1964, Dad's hit "Everybody Loves Somebody," the song that would become his signature, bumped "Hard Day's Night" from the top spot.

"Everybody Loves Somebody" had first been recorded in 1948 by Frank Sinatra, and was co-written by Kenny Lane, Dad's longtime accompanist on piano. The song had never been a hit for Frank, and it had pretty much languished until one rehearsal session when Dad was searching for another song to go on an album. Ken suggested "Everybody Loves Somebody" and Dad figured what the heck, so he recorded it. Later, that first version was filled out with a full orchestra and background singers, and that was the record that America went crazy over in the summer of 1964, just a few months after Dad placed his footprints in concrete at Grauman's Chinese Theater in Hollywood.

In the wake of the hit, a story came out that Dad had discovered Dean-Paul was nuts about the Beatles and their string of hit songs. Telling Dean-Paul that his old man still had his chops, Dad vowed he would record a song that would knock Dean-Paul's beloved Beatles out of the top spot. Hence, the Babe Ruth, call-your-shot legend for Dad's "Everybody Loves Somebody."

The story is repeated in just about every biography or press

Dad leaves his mark in Hollywood's Walk of Fame and we join him in front of Grauman's for the honor: (left to right) Deana, Claudia, Craig, Mom, Gina, Dad, unknown, myself, and Dean-Paul.

account you read of Dad's life. But public relations begets myth begets legend begets history.

I won't say the story about Dad's boast is certainly false. I wasn't in the room when the alleged exchange took place. It was true that Dean-Paul and Deana, like just about every teenager at the time, were into the Beatles. But I never recall Dean-Paul or Dad talking about the wager in later years. Above all, it was not something that would come out of Dad's mouth. He was never an "Oh yeah? Well, I'll just show you" kind of guy. If Dad encountered Dean-Paul raving about John, Paul, George, and Ringo, his response would have been, "Yeah, pallie, the Beatles, whatever." He was certainly comfortable enough in his own skin that he wouldn't have been trying to pull any one-upsmanship to impress us.

I personally believe it was something that the public relations people dreamed up. Rogers & Cowan, the public relations firm that handled the Beatles when they came to tour America, was the same agency that represented Dad, along with Frank Sinatra and other stars. Pitting two clients against each other on the record charts made for a good story that benefited both clients.

If the Beatles had any hard feelings about Dad temporarily knocking them off the top of the charts—they would reclaim the Number One slot just after Christmas in 1964 with "I Feel Fine"—they never let on. Rogers & Cowan hosted a garden party with the Fab Four when they came out to Los Angeles for a concert at the Hollywood Bowl that year and Dad got us all an invitation, although I think he may have skipped the event to go golfing. All of us kids got our picture taken with the Beatles at that party, and the band members were gracious and fun-loving.

Meeting the Beatles was huge for Dean-Paul and Deana. Me, I remember just itching to leave, go home, and get out of my monkey suit. I was 11, and the Beatles didn't hold much relevance in my world, which was still centered around what you could do with a piece of mercury wire, some gunpowder, and an electrical switch.

A decade later, I would meet John Lennon and Ringo Starr again. They were among the guests that Mom pulled in for my twenty-first birthday party at 601 Mountain to celebrate that I had survived my adolescence and was now able to legally drink alcohol—a privilege I remember taking full advantage of that evening. John Lennon always had that certain air of destiny surrounding him, even at a party with Elton John, Kiki Dee, David Bowie, Elizabeth Taylor, Sammy Cahn, Henry Mancini, Arthur Ashe, and Brian and Carl Wilson of the Beach Boys. Ringo, on the other hand, was just your standard-issue lovable goofball.

I remember my band playing a song or two during the party, and then some other people joining in, but unfortunately, much of that night is a blur. I was well-lit and really needed to take a break from the intensity of the celebrity wattage that was milling around. Everywhere you turned, it was people, people, people. Wanting somewhere quiet to decompress for a few minutes, I ducked into the den and shut the door. Peace. I had barely sat down on the couch when the door opened and closed. I turned around to see David Bowie, obviously looking for the same sanctuary as I. He apologized for barging in, and I said no problem and invited him to sit down. We sat and relaxed for awhile, talking about nothing, eventually getting ourselves psyched up to go back out into the churning, noisy waves of partiers. For a fleeting instant, I remember being tempted to go upstairs and climb into bed, calling the Beverly Hills police in a gravelly voice to complain about all the damn noise over at 601.

Of course, the noise at 601 was not confined to parties. Dean-Paul's band would rehearse, audition, and land a recording contract inside 601 Mountain. The trio started not so much due to the Beatlemania that swept America, but more to the musical inspiration that was part of each member's family.

Dean-Paul, who had been exposed to Dad's singing career, came into his own with the rock and roll era. He was always fooling around with a guitar, and he taught himself to play. He bought two of the violin-style Hofner bass guitars that Paul McCartney played in the Beatles, and would later give one of those Beatle basses to Wayne Tweed as a birthday present.

Desi, as the son of Desi Arnaz Sr. (who was Dean-Paul's godfather), had access to all manner of musical instruments and a place to rehearse. While we commandeered a small part of the living room near the bar for rehearsing, Desi had a full-blown stage complete with a lighting and sound system at his house on Whittier. Influenced by his father's "Babaloo Club" on TV, Desi focused on rhythm, playing drums, and percussion.

Billy Hinsche is a great vocalist and can play guitar and piano with equal ease. He was the backbone of Dino, Desi, and

No hard feelings over Dad bumping "A Hard Day's Night" from the top of the record charts. Front row: Gina, myself, Deana, Dean-Paul, and Gail. Back row: George Harrison, John Lennon, Ringo Starr, Paul McCartney, and Mom, 1964.

Billy. He did not come from a show business family, per se. His father, Otto "Doc" Hinsche, ran a sophisticated nightclub in the Philippines before World War II, and when the Japanese invaded, he wound up in a prison camp until Gen. Douglas MacArthur and the Allied forces liberated the Philippines. Doc moved his family to Beverly Hills and made some very shrewd investments in real estate, while Billy went to Beverly Hills Catholic School, where he met Dean-Paul and me. Billy's non-celebrity lineage was always a hitch for introductions or stories about the band, with Doc Hinsche usually referred to as a "prominent Beverly Hills realtor," which indeed he was.

I remember one appearance Dino, Desi, and Billy made on *The Hollywood Palace*, a TV variety show that aired on ABC from 1964 to 1970. Victor Borge was the host, and after the band played, he did a quick interview with them on the air before their second song. First to Dean-Paul, he asked, "And who's your father?"

"Dean Martin," answered Dean-Paul. No reaction from Victor. He moved to Desi next and asked, "And what about your parents, young man?"

"My dad is Desi Arnaz and my mom is Lucille Ball," answered Desi. Again, not even a glimmer of recognition from Victor. Then, to Billy: "And who's your father?"

"Doc Hinsche," said Billy.

"Not *the* Doc Hinsche!" said a suddenly animated Victor. "Really? Doc Hinsche! Can you believe that!" It was a great gag that only Victor Borge could have done.

The way the three of them got together was probably similar to the way most kids form a band, although with a Beverly Hills twist. They start talking at school, and it's, "Well, I play guitar," and "I play the bass," and "I've got a stage," and "My dad's friend owns a record label." Dean-Paul, Desi, and Billy started playing and writing songs and their band started clicking around school. Their first gig was the Beverly Hills Catholic School cotillion, the formal dance held for students.

Mom heard them rehearsing at home one day and decided they might have something, so she called up Frank Sinatra and invited him over to the house to hear an audition. At the time, Frank had his own record label, Reprise Records, which Dad had switched over to and for which he recorded "Everybody Loves Somebody." It was unusual for Frank to be at the house, since he never came over unless it was some sort of special occasion. He sat with Dad at the bar in the living room, where Dean-Paul,

If you had to force it, you weren't singing.

Desi, and Billy had set up their equipment. After the band ran through a few songs, Frank got up from the bar and said, "You boys just got yourselves a record contract."

The commercial debut of Dino, Desi, and Billy in 1965 coincided with Dad's hit parade. Just about every time you turned on a radio that year, it wasn't long before a resident of 601 Mountain was represented. Dad had five top 40 hits that year: "You're Nobody Till Somebody Loves You," "Send Me the Pillow You Dream On," "(Remember Me) I'm the One Who Loves You," "Houston," and "I Will," the latter a top-10 single. In all, the five hits spent twenty-eight weeks in the top 40.

Meanwhile, Dino, Desi, and Billy were giving him a run on the charts. "I'm a Fool" was their biggest hit, peaking at Number 17 and spending seven weeks in the top 40, while "Not the Loving Kind" was the follow-up that spent five weeks in the top 40. Two other songs made the top 100.

Dad and Uncle Mack in the early days, with Mack blissfully unaware one day he would be trampled by stampeding young girls at a Dino, Desi, and Billy concert.

They hit gold at a time when bubble-gum pop was just taking off, and their success spawned plans for a concert tour. Since the budding pop stars were still kids—Dean-Paul and Billy were 14, Desi was 12 years old—Dad decided that Mack Gray would go along on the concert tour and be Dino, Desi, and Billy's manager.

Uncle Mack, of course, had shepherded Dad through hundreds of publicity gigs, movie premieres, public appearances, and trips to Las Vegas. He was the epitome of a celebrity handler, never obtrusive yet always right there to make sure no whacko ever tried something stupid. Dad had complete faith in Mack's ability to keep Dean-Paul and his bandmates out of harm's way.

Nothing could prepare Mack for the prepubescent meltdown and hysteria that accompanied a Dino, Desi, and Billy concert. During a show on the road that Mack managed, at the armory in Washington, D.C., hundreds of screaming teenaged girls rushed the stage during the guys' last song. There were girls climbing over the top of each other for a chance to touch Dino, Desi, and Billy. Mack jumped into the melee, trying to restore order, only to be overrun by the horde of female fans. He was roughed up, trampled, and barely escaped with his life. In the back of the limo as it sped away from the armory, Mack was wheezing and grabbed his chest. "I'm gonna have a heart attack!" he panted.

It was a situation completely foreign to him and he had no idea how to try to control the teeny-bopper stampede. Hoods, tough-guy fans, pushy broads, these were forces he knew how to reckon with. But in a theater full of screeching 12-year-old girls who would allow nothing to stand in the way of touching Dean-Paul's dreamy blonde hair, he was powerless.

I still remember Mom laughing hysterically when Mack came home and announced he was through with being road manager for Dino, Desi, and Billy. He quit. "They took my shoe, my goddamn shoe! Those girls took my shoe and I never found it!" he was ranting. "Never again."

Dad got Bill Howard to take Uncle Mack's place on the Dino, Desi, and Billy tour. Bill was much more accustomed to the puppy-love-gone-rabid scene. He had been our Little League baseball coach, when Dean-Paul and Billy were on the American League of the Beverly Hills Little League. Those late afternoon games were always family affairs at Roxbury Park, with Mom and Dad taking blankets and drinks, sitting in the grandstands, cheering the boys on.

For the guys in the band, the screaming stampede at the close of every show became ridiculous. To avoid the assault, Billy and Dean-Paul liked to play the last song without announcing it as such, then say quick thank yous and jet off the stage. However, as the youngest and therefore the one who got ordered around the most, Desi preferred to have a little fun. In spite of heated admonitions from Billy and Dean-Paul not to say, "Now here's our last song," Desi would inform the crowd that this was indeed their final number as they began playing, squirting gasoline onto the fire.

Although I was never part of the band, I got drawn into the whole bubble-gum scene through articles in magazines like *Tiger Beat* or *Sixteen*, which would run stories under headlines such as "Ricci Tells All on Dino, Desi, and Billy." There would be a photo of me pointing to the guys, and I would reveal some inane personal detail like Billy's favorite food or the kind of girl Dean-Paul liked.

I went along on one leg of their tour and found the whole groupie thing rather frightening. Plus, some of the shows were with other, older bands that provided a glimpse into the hippie hedonism that was waiting just beyond puberty. While Dino, Desi, and Billy headlined many shows, they also ended up opening for bands like Sam the Sham and the Pharaohs, Paul Revere and the Raiders, and the Beach Boys. Many of those band members were shtupping everything in sight, and for young Catholic boys from the somewhat sheltered environs of Beverly Hills, it was definitely eye-opening.

After that first wild year, the band slowly unraveled. They kept recording with modest success, but their music progressively got more experimental, and with lower sales, the options for touring just weren't coming up. Desi's acting career was taking off, and Dean-Paul was getting into the professional tennis circuit. Plus, they were getting older. You don't see many heartthrobs over 17 years old in the pages of *Sixteen*.

I remember when the whole Dino, Desi, and Billy thing came to a halt. Dean-Paul and Billy had been very close friends in forming the band. The two of them had written a song together for Dad to sing, called "For the Love of a Woman," and Dad liked it, as did the people at Reprise. So Dean-Paul and Billy started producing four songs for Dad on his next album, the song they had co-written and three covers of other songs: a tune called "Come On Down"; "Tracks of My Tears," a hit for the Miracles and later for Johnny Rivers and Linda Ronstadt; and "Down Home," which Ricky Nelson had recorded. They were up-tempo numbers, a little more contemporary for Dad, and it seemed like it would be a nice evolution of Dad's sound.

They both went into the studio with Dad in January 1970, and he recorded the four songs, which were pressed into singles. When the box of the first batch of singles came by courier, Billy told me how he opened it up and was devastated when he read the credits on the label: "Produced by Dino Martin Jr." Billy had not gotten any credit, even though he had shared in the production duties. Unbeknownst to Billy, the record company had wanted production credit to go solely to Dean Martin's son, figuring it would help market the songs. Billy came to our house and confronted Dean-Paul about the omission. Billy was so hurt he had tears in his eyes when he left.

When Billy told me about Dean-Paul getting all the credit for producing Dad's new songs, I couldn't believe it and went to Mom to protest. I was young and had never been very assertive, but I could not understand why everyone was agreeing to this dishonesty.

"I know it's not right, but that's what the record company wants and that's what your Dad wants, so that's the way it is," she told me.

I remember walking out of the room stunned, getting my first real taste of how ruthless the music business can be. I was disappointed that Dean-Paul would go along with the marketing ploy to make it look like he had done this alone, when Billy had been an equal part of the project. At the same time, I realized how tough it would have been to stand up to Reprise Records and Dean Martin, our own father. Dean-Paul had been put in an impossible situation.

It was a turning point. While I would go on to record my own album and do a concert tour, I never had the stomach for the music business and have always preferred the technical side of it over the wheeling and dealing. You really have to love the music because the business end of it is the most disheartening, disappointing thing in the world. At the end of the day, all you have is your music. And that doesn't always pay the bills.

Dean-Paul and Billy were never as close after the decision on the production credit for those four songs, which were never included on one of Dad's albums. The episode signaled the final bell for their band. But it never fazed Billy. He was hired right away by the Beach Boys and became a solid part of their band for twenty-five years. He's still one of my dearest friends today.

chapter 7

Dad's Little Jeanne

I never saw Mom jealous of other women, even when they swooned over Dad while around her. It just wasn't an issue. Before she was Mom, she was Dorothy Jean Biegger, a model and queen of the Orange Bowl. She was used to being around beautiful women and wasn't intimidated. Why should she be? She could certainly hold her own, with classic features, perfect blonde hair, and crystal blue eyes. She already had been on magazine covers and soda pop calendars by the time she met Dad in Miami, on New Year's Eve 1948, when she accompanied other Orange Bowl Parade royalty to the Beachcomber's Club to hear that hot new comedy act, Martin and Lewis.

It was a fairy-tale romance, a little make-believe in that Dad made her believe he wasn't married at the time they met. She had not dated much and she, as well as Dad, fell very much in love in those early days. She was 22, ten years younger than Dad, when they were married August 26, 1949.

Maybe at first Mom felt threatened by all the women who adored Dad, but as time went on, I think it was clear she offered him what none of the other girls could—the family. When all my brothers and sisters were under one roof at 601, I think Mom felt that nothing could break up the Martin family.

There were surely a few attempts. Shirley MacLaine was madly in love with Dad, just head over heels. They had worked

"My little Jeanne." Mom at age 21, the fairest of them all. (David Kovar photo)

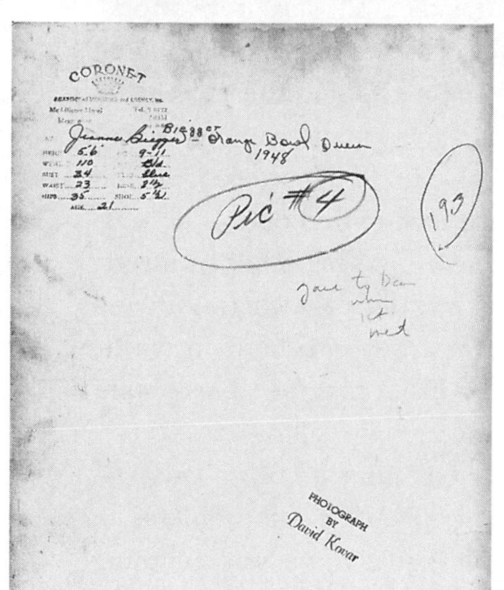

Above: Mom and Dad's first date, Miami Beach, New Year's Eve, 1948.

Left: The back of the 1948 photo, which Mom gave to Dad when they first met, included all her vital statistics.

on some movies, she had dated Frank—didn't they all?—and she was a periodic guest at the parties at 601. In her 1995 book, *My Lucky Stars*, she tells how she could no longer deal with her crush on Dad and decided to tell him that she was in love with him.

Shirley came to the house unexpectedly. She had been there before for parties, but she had never come to 601 during a normal day. Few people did. The only time that we had guests over was during those parties, and it was rare to see any celebrity enter the house solo if there wasn't a party going on.

When Shirley came in, she saw a completely different side

of Dad, one that I suspect she had never really imagined. It was kids jumping on him, the dinner show, all the craziness of a big family. Her image of this guy was based on his professional life: show business, Las Vegas, the Rat Pack, the booze, the singing, the swinger. Even the parties at 601 reinforced that perception. She had never gotten a glimpse of the other side, because Dad took such great pains never to mix family and work. The two were totally separate, except for an occasional joke about his home life in his night club act.

Shirley looked around at this chaos, and she got the whole picture. As much as she loved and cared for Dad, she said she decided right there that this relationship was not something she was going to pursue. She told Dad what a pleasure it was working with him, kissed him on the cheek, and left without giving anybody at 601 a clue as to what she was doing there. She was forever a friend of our family.

There were probably other episodes like that, women who saw Dad as one thing and were surprised to find out his personal world was not as glamorous or romantic as his debonair image. It was your basic nuts-and-bolts family, kids ricocheting in and out of the house, Mom planning her parties and charity projects, and Dad trying to eke out time for his golf game. There were dynamics at home that kept it a sanctuary, for all of us.

At the same time, all the various pursuits of us kids and Mom and Dad may have created a diversion for problems in their marriage. We certainly never knew there was anything wrong or any trouble. I never saw them fight. Sure, you maybe heard a "doggoned it" out of Dad when he walked away, but that would be it. They never argued in front of us kids.

The only time I ever saw Dad irritated at Mom was when he had to wait for her to get ready. Let's say they were going to some function on the town. He would be dressed and ready by a certain designated time and then come down into the living room and wait for Mom. And wait. Thirty minutes, forty-five

Shirley entertaining Dad and Debbie Reynolds on the set.

minutes, sometimes an hour, Dad would sit down there on the couch, smoking, waiting for Jeanne to finally come downstairs so they could leave.

This was always his biggest peeve. It was like his Vegas shows. He wanted to be called twenty minutes before show time so he could get dressed, come down, and start the thing when the thing was supposed to start. He didn't like getting ready and then sitting around. "Just give me a time," he'd say to Mom if they were going out. He didn't care if it was 8:00 or 9:00, but he would fume if she said 7:00 and didn't come down until 8:00. He could have watched television in bed for another forty-five minutes if that was the case.

Waiting was one of those things Dad endured, and I don't think Mom ever understood. She loved the nightlife, and even if

Mr. and Mrs. Martin,
the early 1950s.
(Bud Fraker photo)

Dad had been working all day, she didn't really consider what he did all day exactly "work." She had been to the movie sets, the TV shows. Everyone just lounges around until they set the shot; you do your lines and in a couple of minutes it's back to your trailer.

But that waiting around can drive you mad. I know what it's like to make a movie and it is not fun. I did a movie in Maui in 1983 with Lisa Hartman and Bobby Hegyes. It was called *Tell Me That You Love Me*, a teen flick in which I played a thief. When they screened it for a test audience, one of the audience members wrote on the comment card, "Just tell me it's over." It was horrid, a real bomb.

Of course, one night many years later, Dad was over at Mom's house and he said, "Pallie, were you ever in a movie?" When I told him yes, Dad said, "I think I saw it on TV last night at about 3 A.M."

Yeah, Dad, that was me. Just tell me it's over.

But from my experience with movie-making, I understood what it was like to sit there with tissue tucked into your shirt collar so you don't get makeup on your shirt, waiting until they set the shot and light it. Then you go out, do your four minutes, and resume waiting while they set up the next shot. You spend most of your day waiting, and it's a pain in the ass, nothing glamorous at all about it.

Stage gigs were the same thing. All day long, there's really nothing much to do in a hotel room except watch TV. All that waiting around for a ninety-minute show each night. But that was the deal in the business Dad was in. He endured it at work, but waiting around was the last thing he wanted to do at home.

Over time, Mom and Dad's clocks seemed to get more out of sync, and I have always felt, in essence, that's why things didn't work out for them. Mom loved her parties, her nightlife, and her friends, and she would still be in full hostess mode at 1 A.M. on a weeknight. It was always funny that Dad had this image of

Opposites attract. Myself, Dad, Gina, Mom, and Dean-Paul, seeing if we could all fit onto one couch in the living room at 601 in 1967.

the guy who never leaves the bar when it was Mom who could have led the dawn patrol over the Rat Pack. Mom was a night owl and a late sleeper. Dad, on the other hand, was an early riser and, therefore, early to bed. Complete opposites. When one was running on all cylinders, the other was in bed. Or at least wanted to be.

Mom frequently failed to understand why Dad could be so tired early in the evening. One of her favorite zingers to him when he would groan about going out at night because he was tired was, "Oh, tough day golfing, dear?"

She had him there, to a point. Anyone who golfs knows that doing eighteen holes takes a little out of you. But Dad did his eighteen without a cart. He walked it. There were days when he

The early riser gets the first tee time. Dad, October 1958, at the Bel-Air Country Club. (Allan Grant photo)

would walk twenty-seven or even thirty-six holes. It was his exercise and his favorite thing to do.

In the early days, golfing in Beverly Hills was a little tricky because scions of southern California's land and water barons controlled the country club courses. The old money crowd looked down on club membership for Jews, blacks, and people in the entertainment industry. It wasn't long, however, before those establishment barriers broke down. New or old, the color of money is the same. At one time, Dad considered developing his own upscale country club and golf course on property between Benedict Canyon Drive and Coldwater Canyon Drive. But he would rather play a course than plan it.

People always wondered if Dean Martin's tan was stage makeup or from a heat lamp. It was the real thing. When you walk eighteen holes of golf in Beverly Hills nearly every day, you get a nice tan. You also come home damn bent. Plus, after golf, Dad would invariably have a few cocktails with his friends, so he would come home ready to relax. Mom might sleep until 10 A.M. or 11 A.M., while Dad was well into his golf game.

One revving up, one winding down. Over time, their relationship deteriorated because of that. Things do change that way, but there was never any visible acrimony between them. As kids, we didn't recognize any change in the way they treated each other, even if things had changed for them personally. I found out later that Dad had wanted out of the marriage to Mom in about 1963, when I was 10 and Gina, the youngest of our family, was 6. Mom and Dad later told me that they decided they did not want her to have one parent growing up, so they would wait until she was older before they got divorced.

We never knew. We still felt genuine, immense love from both of them. It was not as if we were living in some sort of charade, because there wasn't any phoniness or animosity between them. There was a definite friendship, maybe even an accommodation. When he would come home, he'd give his "Little

Off to Las Vegas, 1958. Dad, Mom, Claudia, Gail, Deana, Dean-Paul, myself, and Gina.

Jeanne" a kiss, and then they would both go about their normal routines. As we grew up and everyone was doing their own thing, the only time we would come together as a family was for dinner every night, and that's when we were just crazy and laughing and feeling good.

There was a great harmony between Mom and Dad, even though you were never really seeing them together all lovey-dovey in the later years. But you also were never seeing them apart, because they were going out together, coming in together, and, in their own way, seemed to be content.

Dad was still worth a few surprises. I remember coming home one day and walking through the kitchen to find him cutting up some thick New York steaks on the butcher block. Whoa! Outside of him buttering a slice of bread, you never saw Dad in the kitchen. He never cooked. Never even fried an egg. I remember saying to Gina, in perhaps the same manner Dad had asked Mom about the tank in the garage, "Was that *Dad* I saw in the kitchen?"

He had been on location in the Southwest for one of his western movies and someone on the chuck wagon crew showed him a special way to cook New York steaks on the grill. So Dad came home and announced he was cooking tonight, going to use the barbecue. Once our cook, Alma, regained consciousness, Dad had her get him some thick New York steaks. He cut three diagonal slits in each of the steaks. Then he put them in a baking pan, poured olive oil over them, and began massaging the meat with his big hands, working the oil into the slices he made in each steak.

By now, the entire household was in the kitchen, watching this historic event. I'm thinking, call Guinness. Dad took the steaks out to the barbecue, which was full of glowing charcoal briquettes, and started slapping the meat down on the grill. Each time a steak would make contact, the oil would burst into flame, searing the flavor in. We were still not sure what was the bigger

Mom would later give her pearl and diamond ring to my wife, Annie.

spectacle—the towers of fire or seeing Dad with a big barbecue fork in his hand.

The steaks were delicious and became a staple of the family menu, to the point that the staff took over the preparation and I assumed grilling duties, allowing Dad to retire from his brief but illustrious culinary career.

If he was unhappy with their marriage, Dad never let on to us. He would still buy Mom gifts. In the early days, he bought her a beautiful pearl and diamond ring. The joke was always, "Fortunately, the finger wasn't still in it."

We did have one clue that something was a little bit differ-

Mom and Dad in Rome, about 1955.

ent at 601 when Mom and Dad changed their sleeping arrangements. Dad had an office just off their bedroom, and one day we noticed he had moved a small bed and a television into that office. The walls were decorated with his western stuff, the guns and posters and things, not the pinks and powder blues that Mom had decorated their bedroom with. At the foot of the bed, facing the door as you came in, Dad had placed a life-sized, six-foot-tall, mechanically animated cowboy gunslinger which someone had given him. The outlaw looked just like a real person, and when the arcade game was turned on, his voice would say, "OK, draw!" and you would try to shoot him with a beam of light from your pistol before the gunslinger raised his own six-shooter.

Shortly after Dad installed the gunslinger in his new bedroom, Irma, our usually unflappable housekeeper, walked into the room to straighten up. The quick-draw game had been left on, and before she could flip on the light switch, the gunslinger grunted, "OK, draw!" and his arm raised, the toy gun drawing a bead on Irma. She nearly died from fright. Even when she found out it was just a mechanical toy that was pulling a gun on her, she avoided Dad's bedroom for quite a while after that.

We never thought too much about Dad and Mom sleeping in different rooms because it seemed to make sense with their different waking and sleeping cycles. Dad would wake up earlier and go to bed earlier than Mom, plus he liked to watch shows on TV like westerns that Mom never cared for, so we just figured it was for convenience, wanting their separate space. Even though they had agreed to live separate lives under the same roof, I don't think either one of them was convinced that their marriage was over during those years. There were truly feelings there, but they had a difficult time getting closer.

Dad's ranch-style bedroom may have prompted Mom to buy him the full-scale version, the 64-acre Hidden Valley Ranch near Thousand Oaks in Ventura County. Friends later said that the ranch was Mom's last-ditch effort to save their marriage by building Dad a place she thought he would really love, sort of his own "Ponderosa Ranch" from one of his favorite TV shows, *Bonanza*. Of course, the first time we saw it in 1968, it looked like a ghost town. Call it the "Almosta Ranch."

As you drove in through the main gate, there was a windmill that, in the old days, ran a generator for the electricity to the ranch house. The big house was a shambles, but it surrounded a center courtyard and an old broken fountain. There were garages off to the left of the house, and then a smaller house set right against a hillside near the garage.

That little house had a big wooden door, and when you went inside, you found a foot-thick bank-vault door leading into a room that was actually dug into the side of the mountain. The walls were lined with shelves notched for bottle necks. The real

Ranch hands at Hacienda Martin, November 1968: (back row) Wayne Tweed, Spencer Segura, Dean-Paul, Jay Judson, Ned Wynn, myself, Billy Hinsche, Luci Arnaz; (front row) Gina, Karen Hoffman, Ursula Andress, Mom, and Desi Arnaz Jr. (Jean-Claude Killy photo)

estate agent giving us a tour said the place had been built years ago by gangsters who stored liquor in the cave during Prohibition. I remember turning to Dean-Paul at the time and saying, "Cool."

Around the left side of the house there was another depression in the rock hillside, with a concrete wall arcing out from the mountain, the wall lined with a picket of steel bars curved in at the top. The real estate agent said that this had been a bear cage, where the rum runners had kept several bears that were used to patrol the property and intercept any "revenuers" who might come sniffing around.

Guard bears. We turned to Mom and said, "Mom, this is it."

We got the ranch, sans bears. However, Mom did put in just about everything else, including two years of work and a lot of money. The entire house was gutted and rebuilt, with huge beamed ceilings, tiled floors, big leather couches, and a remote-controlled camera security system. She built new stables so we could bring Dad's favorite horse from his movies, Tops, out to the ranch.

The courtyard was repaved and the fountain rebuilt to hold flowers. A bridge to the left led to a new swimming pool, while to the right Mom put in a tennis court. Up a rise from the swimming pool, a heliport was built, with two fueling stations, one for the regular high-octane aviation fuel and another for jet fuel. At the time, Dean-Paul had begun taking helicopter-flying lessons and was planning on graduating up to a Bell JetRanger, so he convinced Mom to put in a jet-fuel station at the ranch.

There was a big pond and then a small valley that Mom had landscaped and planted as a full chip-and-putt golf course for Dad. It was immaculate and idyllic. One of the putting greens of that golf course was where I took a picture of the Beach Boys that wound up on the cover of one of their record albums. I was still in high school at Rexford, and since my profession at the time was as a photographer on Dad's television show, I invited the Beach Boys out to the ranch for a photo session. We went out to the golf course and they lounged around on the grass, playing with their kids. It was a sunny day, and the photos turned out great. One of the shots on the golf course became the cover art for *Sunflower*, their 1970 album.

A few months later, Carl Wilson and his wife at the time, Annie (Billy Hinsche's sister), called up and said, "We have a surprise for you." They picked me up in their car, and we took the roundabout way onto Sunset Boulevard, heading west toward the Strip. Along the way, there was a huge billboard of the album cover photo I had taken, promoting *Sunflower*. It was a nice thank you.

Unfortunately, about the time Mom got the ranch finished, her marriage to Dad was pretty much over. It was late in 1969 when Mom told me that Dad was moving out of the house and the two were going to get a divorce. By that time, I had started to notice the distance between Mom and Dad. She wanted me to

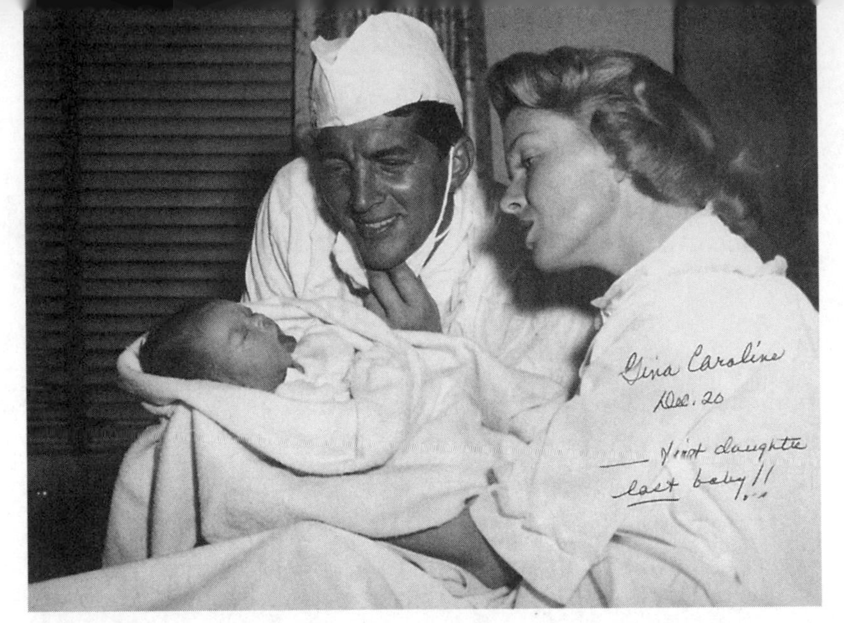

Dad and Mom and newborn Gina, December 1956. Mom has written: "First daughter, last baby!"

tell Gina, knowing that Gina would take it very hard. Part of the problem was that there had been no outward signs that Mom and Dad were not getting along, so the news would come as a shock.

All the same, I don't remember being devastated by Mom's announcement. I was 17, in high school, with my own car. The 1970s were dawning, and it was all groovy, I guess. I had separate relationships with each of them, and I knew I would still see them both regularly. In fact, Dad was going to live nearby, in Bel Air. He'd have his house, Mom would have the house at 601, and if they were both going to be happier apart, I didn't seem to have a problem with their divorce.

I told Mom, "Sure, no problem, I'll tell Gina." By this time, all the older girls, Claudia, Gail, and Deana, had moved out of the house, as had Craig. Dean-Paul was nearly married to Olivia Hussey and was in the midst of moving out into his new home. So Gina and I were the two children left at 601 when Mom and Dad decided to get divorced.

The news was especially rough on Gina. Try as I might to rationalize how this was really a good thing for everybody, that we would still be a family and that Mom and Dad would be happier living apart, Gina was devastated. Many years later I talked to her about that conversation we had and realized she had blocked out much of our discussion. She even thought Dean-Paul had been the one to tell her about Mom and Dad's divorce.

Seeing her sobbing that day after I told her the news gave me pause. Maybe I was taking it too lightly, this whole divorce thing. We were used to the routine with Mom and Dad, and even though all of us were growing up and flying the nest, there was a tremendous amount of comfort in knowing that there was a family dinner at 601 Mountain every night. Now, I started to realize those times were probably gone.

I spent a lot of time out at the ranch during those days. Although it had been restored into an immaculate showpiece, Mom hardly ever came out, and Dad visited just once or twice. His focus was somewhere else. It had been Mom's pride and joy, and here I was, partying with my friends, drinking, riding motorcycles, shooting guns, driving the tank around. It was an incredible party place, but an air of sadness drifted around it. Mom's dreams for it were never quite realized.

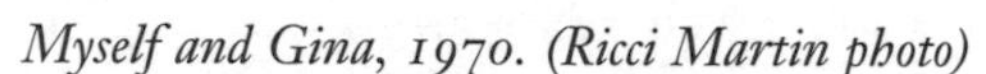

Myself and Gina, 1970. (Ricci Martin photo)

One day on my way out to the ranch, I was pulled over for speeding. More often than not, being the child of a celebrity works against you. In the old days, we kept some of our season tickets to the Dodgers games in the glove box of the car, along with a supply of "Dino" pens. The pens were ballpoints that were made for Dad, and they came in two styles, each with a "Dino!" logo. One said, "This pen is cute but you can't drink it." The other read, "It's Frank's world and we're just living in it." Usually, a couple of Dodger tickets and some Dino pens helped ease the tension of a speeding pullover.

But this time, when the police officer checked the registration and saw Dad's name as the lien holder, he handed back my license and registration and said, "Son, I'm sorry to hear about your parents getting a divorce. I'm sure you've got a lot on your mind these days. Slow down a little, and I hope everything works out for your family."

I was stunned by my good fortune. But the cop was right, even if I didn't want to recognize it. I did have a lot on my mind. There was an end of the innocence, and no matter how friendly and logical it all seemed, I was confronted with the stark realization that Mom and Dad were getting a divorce.

The divorce actually took three years from the time it became public in January 1970. Dad didn't file the petition for another two years, in 1972, and when the settlement was finally reached in 1973, their breakup made the news again. I remember walking into school when the thing was over and somebody ribbing me about my parents being in the *Guinness Book of Records*. I thought they were kidding, but then someone showed me the listing for most expensive divorce settlement, Dean Martin from Jeanne Martin.

Dad had told his lawyers, "Give her what she wants." Of course, the lawyers were saying no, Dean, no. But Dad was adamant. So the settlement was a whopper, something like $6.5 million. Mom got the house, some of the cars, and other prop-

Separate, but never apart. Dad and myself in 1976 at his Bel Air house after the divorce.

erty, plus a sizable portion of Dad's production company, which was merged into NBC and converted into RCA stock.

All of us kids maintained good but separate relationships with Mom and Dad. They quit speaking to each other and there were no such things as family gatherings or dinners anymore. I think it was a mutually imposed silence and isolation. Mom was obviously hurt. I never found myself choosing sides and placing blame. I loved them both for who they were, and they played equal parts in making me the person I am today. Dad never talked about his divorce from Mom, which wasn't too surprising to me. That was his style, that old Italian code, just walk away and never look back. He had done it with Jerry years earlier and now he was doing it with Mom.

Even for Dad, though, there are some people you just can't turn your back on forever. He should have known by now. He had sung that damn song so many times.

Everybody loves somebody sometime.

chapter 8

The Big Clam

Shortly after Mom and Dad announced they were getting a divorce, a pair of detectives from the Los Angeles Police Department showed up at the door of 601 Mountain and asked Mom if they could talk to me about Charles Manson. As if she didn't have enough to worry about.

The Tate-LaBianca murders had stunned the world late in the summer of 1969, when the Manson cult "family" had murdered actress Sharon Tate and four others at a house in Benedict Canyon and then killed supermarket chain president Leno LaBianca and his wife at their Los Angeles home later the same weekend. Police at first said the killings were unrelated, but eventually, a jury convicted Manson and several of his followers of all seven murders, giving them death sentences later commuted to life imprisonment.

I was 17 at the time, and the threads that connected me to the hippie Manson family were thin, but the LAPD was in the process of checking out every angle as it worked with prosecutors to build a case against Manson, who had not physically been at the Tate home during the murders. I sat down with the detectives and they showed me pictures of members of his group, asking me what I knew. It wasn't much. My familiarity to Manson's racist cult group was through Dennis Wilson of the Beach Boys. Dennis, who had dabbled in the whole psychedelic scene, had been approached by Manson to record some of his songs—Charlie thought of himself as an accomplished guitarist and songwriter, and his followers considered him a neglected musical genius. He was always pestering Dennis to record his songs and help him get a record deal. I had heard Manson's songs and I wasn't impressed.

I never met Manson or his family when they were hanging out at Dennis's place, although Billy Hinsche, who had joined the Beach Boys band after Dino, Desi, and Billy broke up, did. At one point, I think Billy even gave me a coat from Linda Kasabian, the family member who later acted as lookout on that horrible night in Benedict Canyon.

The house on Cielo Drive that Sharon Tate was living in at the time of the murders was owned by Rudi Altobelli, a Hollywood manager for several prominent stars, including Olivia Hussey and, later, Dean-Paul. Rudi rented the main house to Sharon and her husband, director Roman Polanski (who was out of town the night of the killings), while he periodically stayed in the guesthouse. Rudi had bought the house from Doris Day's son, Terry Melcher, who had briefly dated my older sister Claudia.

This is how it seemed at the time in Beverly Hills. Everybody knew everybody or knew someone who knew someone else. It was a small town.

Manson had come to the Cielo Drive house looking for Terry a few months before the murders, hoping that Terry would be a financial backer for his recording dream. Dennis Wilson had suggested Terry to Manson, trying to get Charlie out of his hair. Like Dennis, Terry found nothing worth producing in Manson's songs, and both drew the intense resentment of the Manson family as a result.

At one point, several members of that hippie crowd warned the Beach Boys that Charlie had ordered a hit on them because Dennis had not helped Manson make his recording fantasy a reality. When there were rumors of it actually happening on a certain night, I remember going over to Carl Wilson's house in Coldwater Canyon with Billy, whose sister Annie had married Carl.

I brought along a couple of pieces from Dean-Paul's machine-gun collection, and Billy and I sat up all night in Carl's living room with the automatics in our lap, watching and waiting, just in case the rumored hit was true. I remember that as a very long, tense night. Strange times.

One of the psychiatrists brought in by investigators to evaluate the sanity of Manson was Dr. Andre Tweed, Wayne's father. Eventually, as Manson's twisted "helter skelter" murder plans unfolded in courtroom testimony, several famous friends of ours were discovered on the Manson family hit list, including Frank Sinatra. Sharon Tate had been one of Dad's co-stars in his last Matt Helm film, *The Wrecking Crew*, in 1969. So the whole Manson thing was way too close for comfort.

Years later, I learned that at about this time, Dad notified the FBI about a letter he had received. In all capital letters, the typewritten note read, in part: "My dear hip Mr. Martin. This is a letter that will be short & brief. 'Life' or the Unknown. Your son has been hanging around with the wrong crowd. Sharon Tate has friends. You've got a nice wife and kids too. If you want to keep them in good health or maybe just part of their health, you'll do the following or face the consequences."

Full of misspellings and mangled syntax, the letter from "The Sharon Tate Fan Club" went on to demand $3,000 be sent to an address in Vancouver, Washington. On a second page, it threatened to kill Dad's mom. At the time, Angela had been dead nearly five years.

While crank letters were a periodic occurrence in Dad's fan mail, this one was a bit unusual because of the Sharon Tate reference. The FBI opened a case file on the letter, but their report noted that Dad suspected it was a juvenile because of the demand

Another fashion victim of the 1970s. Me, in 1972, at age 19, leaving Jack Hansen's Daisy Club on Rodeo Drive in Beverly Hills. (Frank Edwards photo)

of only $3,000. The FBI wrote that Dad "said the letter caused him no concern for his own safety, but caused him a little apprehension on behalf of his mother who resides with him." I suspect they misunderstood that he was concerned for Peggy, Mom's mother.

When Olivia Hussey moved from London to California to be closer to Dean-Paul after they started dating, Rudi had her stay in the Cielo Drive house, last occupied by Sharon Tate. Dean-Paul spent a lot of time at that house with Olivia, before they were married and moved to their own home. Naturally, you couldn't see any trace of the murders. But the place definitely gave me the creeps.

While Dean-Paul was wooing Olivia—he had seen her in the 1968 movie *Romeo and Juliet* and fallen immediately in love—most of my other brothers and sisters were starting families of their own. Gail had graduated from college in England and in 1968 married a lawyer, Paul Polena. They had two daughters, Cappy and Liza. Craig, who was never into singing and acting, moved from his work in the production side of Dad's TV show into other jobs behind the scenes, producing everything from variety to cartoon shows. He would later hire me for a syndicated television program he produced, *The Rock Show*, which was a precursor to the arrival of MTV. Thanks to Craig, I was perhaps the first "vee-jay" in Los Angeles, introducing music videos and then doing a little comedy routine in between songs for the show, which aired late at night weekly in the L.A. market.

Craig had married Sandy Pfiffer when he was in the army, and they had two children. After they divorced, he married one of the dancers from Dad's TV show, Kami Stevens, in 1969. The same year, Claudia married an actor named Keil Mueller, who changed his named to Keil Martin. They had a daughter, Jesse, and Keil went on to play Detective J. D. LaRue for many seasons on the TV show *Hill Street Blues*.

A few weeks after Claudia's wedding, Deana jumped in and

married Terry Guerin, a writer. Dean-Paul wed Olivia Hussey in 1971 and they had a son, Alexander. So, while Mom and Dad were ending their marriage of twenty years, the kids were doing their best to keep the wedding bells ringing. But Gina and I, the youngest of the brood, were in no hurry to join in.

Most of the older kids managed to dabble in show business a little, then escape to lead pretty normal lives. Claudia had movie roles in *For Those Who Think Young* (1964), *The Girl in the Invisible Bikini* (1966), and *Ski Fever* (1967), plus appeared in episodes of the TV shows *My Three Sons* and *The Donna Reed Show*. Deana had a role in a 1968 episode of *The Monkees* TV show, then had parts in two 1969 movies, *Strangers at Sunrise* and *Young Billy Young*.

Dean-Paul had uncredited roles in two of Dad's films, *Murderers' Row*, a Matt Helm sequel in 1966, and *Rough Night in Jericho*, a western the following year. He won the lead in John Derek's 1969 movie, *A Boy . . . a Girl*, which literally was a stinker. The night of its premiere, there was a strike of union theater workers underway and someone put a stink bomb in the air-conditioning system of the theater to protest the use of non-union workers. Not even halfway through Dean-Paul's new movie, the theater emptied out due to the smell.

Dean-Paul would later play opposite Ali MacGraw in the tennis romance *Players* in 1979. That film earned Dean-Paul a 1980 nomination for a Golden Globe for "New Male Star of the Year in a Motion Picture." Gail had numerous appearances singing on Dad's TV show and the summer replacement series, plus she was performing at various clubs in the early 1970s.

I had never been that interested in the acting or singing growing up; I was more into guns and motorcycles and blowing things up. But after Wayne Tweed and I starting hanging out, we began messing around with songwriting and playing music, and eventually we put together a band with his brother, Roland. Wayne was an excellent bass player—he would go on to play

Olivia Hussey and Dean-Paul.

with Smokey Robinson's band for a dozen years. Roland was a keyboardist, and I played drums.

It was one of those things that just sort of evolved. I continued to play and write songs after I graduated from high school and began film school at the California Institute of the Arts at Valencia College. One afternoon, up at Carl Wilson's house, I was playing one of my songs on his piano. It was called "Stop, Look Around." Carl came out of the bedroom and said, "That's good. I'd like to record that."

We went into the studio and recorded the song, and it turned out great. If it was going to be a single, I needed a "B" side, so we recorded another one of my songs. Then Carl said, "Let's record an album."

It took three years. Carl and Billy produced the album, *Beached*, and I managed to get some outstanding people to join in on it with me, like Peter Cetera from the group Chicago, Gerry Beckley of America, Van Dyke Parks, Dennis Wilson of the Beach Boys, and Jimmy McCulloch from Wings, to name just a few. Once *Beached* was completed, the Beach Boys invited me to join the East Coast and Canadian portion of their 1978 concert tour as the opening act. It was an incredible, humbling experience, playing Central Park for a quarter-million people.

I stayed with the Beach Boys through the rest of their North American tour. But while I was promoting the album in concerts, the record company failed to get behind it and market it to radio programmers. Without airplay, it stiffed. Even if people heard songs from *Beached* at the concerts and wanted to buy the album in a record store, chances were they couldn't find it because the record company hadn't supplied the stores. *Beached* ran aground before it had even been untied from the dock.

In spite of my disappointment over the album, I continued playing the club circuit in Los Angeles and indulging in the night life that came along with it. One evening, I was invited by my longtime friend, actress Melanie Griffith, to the premier of *The Blue Lagoon*, the Brooke Shields movie. After the movie, we went to La Dome, a restaurant on Sunset Boulevard, with Annie Lockhart, June Lockhart's daughter. Leaving the restaurant, Melanie and I crossed Sunset Boulevard holding hands.

Out of nowhere, a car ran through the crosswalk, brushed the back of my legs, and hit Melanie. The front of the car struck her hip in mid-stride, whiplashing her head back into the windshield. As the car screeched to a stop, Melanie catapulted more than a dozen feet forward into the curbside, hitting with great force.

I immediately ran to her, calling her name, but she was

Ali MacGraw, Dean-Paul, and Bob Evans on the set of the 1979 movie Players.

unresponsive and her eyes were closed. I saw some blood trickling from her mouth, and at that moment I thought for sure she had been killed. Fortunately, she began moaning. Melanie was rushed to the hospital. She had serious injuries, but she recovered and went on to a great acting career, although I'm sure to this day, she still must experience pain from that accident.

While we kids were chasing dreams in all directions, Mom and Dad had stopped speaking. I believe the last time they were seen together in public was during Dean-Paul's wedding. During those years, we got into a routine of spending time at Dad's house and then going over to Mom's, never discussing one with the other.

Dad had begun dating Gail Renshaw almost immediately after he moved out of 601, although that romance was over in a matter of months. Dad had his freedom, and there was no way he was going to get back into another marriage right off the bat. He eventually met Kathy Hawn, a receptionist at a Beverly Hills hair salon, and she and Dad moved in to a house in Bel Air with her daughter, Sasha.

Dad had been introduced to Kathy by Frank Calcagnini, a friend of the family. Frank was one of the few men Mom dated after her divorce from Dad. She certainly had suitors: Howard Hughes inquired about her, and William Shatner wanted to date her, but Mom always said, "No way." This was a little bit of self-imposed exile on her part. Still the gracious hostess, she threw big parties at 601, with dozens of famous faces, but she was never into the dating scene.

Frank Calcagnini and I were good friends. He was about twenty years younger than Mom, and he would call Mom "Biegs," short for her last name. She would refer to him as

Main Squeeze, one of the tightest bands I was ever in during the early 1980s, whose members went on to play for great headliners. (left to right) Wayne Tweed (Smokey Robinson), Billy Hinsche (Beach Boys), myself, Steve Ross (Stevie Nicks), Ricky Fataar (Bonnie Rait), Carly Munoz (Beach Boys), and Sammy Clayton (Little Feat). (Wayne Williams photo)

"Calcagnini." They were endearing and exasperating to each other, periodically having some lively arguments. "Biegs is driving me crazy!" Frank would say after exiting the house to the sound of a door slamming behind him. He would drive Mom equally nuts. Frank eventually was engaged to Jackie Collins, the novelist, before dying too young at age 51 of cancer.

I had moved out of 601 Mountain just before I started working with Carl Wilson and Billy on my album, and with Gina out on her own—skating in the Ice Capades—it was just Mom living there amid so many memories of the great years with the family and Dad. She eventually decided to sell the house at 601, finding a new house just up Loma Vista on Robert Lane near Greystone Park. Mom decided to remodel her new house. While the work was underway, she rented a house nearby.

The ranch in Thousand Oaks also was sold, first to one of Dad's golfing buddies, Fletcher Jones, a Los Angeles car dealer, then later to Tom Selleck, the actor. Tops, Dad's horse that had stayed at the ranch while not being ridden in one of his movies, died unexpectedly during the filming of *Showdown* in 1972. Tops was 18 years old. Dad was equal parts sad and angry over Tops's death, which was caused by a worker on the production who had given Tops the wrong feed. Many years later, I would memorialize Tops by borrowing his name for a miniature horse we received from Joan Conrad—the daughter of actor Robert Conrad of TV's *Wild, Wild West* fame—as thanks for doing a recording session for her son.

After Dad and Kathy married, the television show began a transition from a variety format to celebrity roasts. I was still there, working as a staff photographer for Greg Garrison, the show's producer. The show lost much of its spontaneity during that transition. Although the roasts were initially shot with a live audience, much of what was seen on TV came from segments shot after the audience was released. Many of the jokes and the reactions were filmed in different takes. The production team would bring in one celebrity, sit the person at the dais, and then take a tight shot as the person delivered lines to nobody or to stand-ins. Then they'd edit in the other takes of stars reacting. It was hollow compared to the earlier days of the show, and it was obvious Dad wasn't himself. Greg's standard line during those shoots was, "Hey, the [laugh] machine will love it." Perhaps none too soon, the show had its final season.

Dad, who was approaching age 60, had started to ease into retirement. But one day, at his house in Bel Air, he was talking to me about a new car he was going to buy. He called his business office to check about some detail, and one of the accountants in the office told him, "Dean, you've only got $250 in the bank." Dad was stunned. While he had a lot of money on paper—real estate, stocks, bonds, and notes—his liquid funds had disappeared.

Dad was always very trusting with his business people, and this time that trust had been taken advantage of, because there had been a serious mishandling of his funds. With his closest associates, he had no written financial contracts; most of them probably worked on a handshake deal. When he agreed to play the MGM Grand, he did not sign a contract, just gave them his word, which was his bond. That was unheard of in Las Vegas—a headliner at a major casino who did not work under contract. But Dad's reputation was such that people who did business with him trusted him. They had an understanding; they would watch out for Dad's interests and he would take care of them.

Rarely would you see Dad write a check. He didn't need to. Most of his travel expenses were taken care of in advance—the hotels, limos, and plane tickets. He would rarely go out, so he seldom had to sign for something. If he did, he'd sign the slip, the bill would be sent to the house, and a secretary would cut a check and pay for it. Dad mainly carried cash for tips, and in the

later days of Las Vegas, at the MGM Grand and Bally's, he and Frank became legendary as tippers. It was nothing for them to hand a waitress or parking valet a hundred-dollar bill.

Of course, they each had their own distinctive styles to tipping. With Dad, it was very low key, like "Thanks, pallie." With Frank, it was more like, "You ever got a tip that big before?" Or "Here! Go out and buy yourself a new wife!"

Now, when Dad was hoping to scale back his schedule, he was forced to go back to work to replenish that empty cash account rather than start selling off assets. It was a tough time for him, and I know he was unhappy with the turn of events. A few weeks later, Dad asked me what might be a good car to buy, not very pricey but something he might like. I told him Gina had an Alfa Romeo Spider convertible and she loved it, so he ended up getting a silver Alfa with black interior. A short time later, one of his friends saw him drive up in the Alfa and asked him why he was driving his kid's car. Dad never drove the Alfa again.

About this time, Dad strained his back badly on the golf course, an injury that would gradually slow him down and deteriorate his health. There had been a period earlier when he went through pills, Percodan, which was a problem in Hollywood for a lot of people. Jerry Lewis, Judy Garland, and others had problems with Percodan, because in those days no one understood about the addiction. Percodan was taken as if it was aspirin. Most of the time, it was a dentist who had prescribed the drug.

Dad divorced Kathy in 1976 but wanted to make sure Sasha, whom he had adopted and we considered our sister, was taken care of. He had set up an office for his accountant, Ellie, whom he trusted and was a close friend of the family. She took over his business affairs and managed to turn his financial problems around.

I never knew how it happened, or who made the first phone

Opposite: Dad meeting Prince Charles while Cary Grant looks on.

call (I suspect it was Dad), but some time later, in about 1982, Mom called me and asked me for a favor.

"Dad's coming over to visit and I wish you'd be here, Ricci," she said. I was stunned. The two of them had literally not seen each other for ten years and, to my knowledge, had seldom if ever spoken to each other during that time. After I got my breath back, I said, "Wow. Well, OK, sure. I'll be there."

I was thrilled.

Mom's newly remodeled house on Robert Lane looked simple from the outside—just a beige adobe home on a hill, behind a wall with two Art Deco gates. You entered by a walkway, past sculptured bushes and shrubs, coming to a pair of towering wooden front doors.

Inside, the entrance was made of sand-colored marble floors and stucco walls painted eggshell that rose to the 20-foot ceilings. Beautiful artwork and murals decorated the walls, and a sunken rectangular marble fountain stood in the middle of the foyer, with small, arcing sprays of water on each side, colliding above the center of the pool. Directly ahead was a formal living room, all in white with an ebony grand piano. On the left side was the dining room with an attached living room and sunken bar.

Straight through the formal living room was a huge glass window that looked directly onto a dark-bottom swimming pool that stretched 35 feet long, more like a wide lap pool. Mom never liked the look of a diving board; she thought it was too sporty. Instead, where you might normally see the diving board, there was a rare giant clam shell, an amazing relic from the ocean floor that was about four feet across, mounted on a granite pedestal. It was mounted so the shell was partially open, and spotlights were arranged to show it off as the museum piece it was. Behind the giant clam, a panorama of Beverly Hills and L.A. stretched out below.

It was an incredible place, just gorgeous, no expense spared. And Dad was paying a visit. I went over to Mom's house to be the official greeter for this historic détente in the post-divorce Cold War era. Mom was in her bedroom when Dad arrived, and I let him in the door. He walked into that marble foyer, his boots clicking in the old rhythmic pattern that we knew so well from 601, his eyes taking in this flamboyant spectacle of interior decorating.

After a minute of gazing around, he stopped, looked at me, grinned, and said: "So. This is where all my money went."

Mom came out of her room and the two of them sat down at the bar while I mixed them both a drink. I stayed for a short time after serving, then I left the room and went off into another part of the house. Later, I was pleasantly surprised to find Dad was still there and they were still talking. I don't know what their conversation was about, but that day marked a new chapter for our family.

From then on, Mom and Dad were friends again. They rekindled their relationship on terms they could both live with, and we began seeing them together on a regular basis, having dinners usually on Sundays at Mom's with some of us kids, and, by now, grandkids.

Mom didn't live too long at Robert Lane. Transforming that house into a showpiece had drained much of her resources, an estimated $5 million, and she had sold a big chunk of her RCA stock to pay for it. When Dad found out about that he told me, "Pallie, I wish I had known because I would have bought that stock back from her. She should never have sold it. She should have borrowed on it."

I believe Mom also regretted getting involved in such a money pit. The fights she had with contractors almost gave her a nervous breakdown, and when the whole thing was done, the house was so huge, I think it must have been lonely.

But before she sold it to actress Pia Zadora and her billionaire husband, Meshulam Riklis, I used it as an emergency backdrop for Dad's one and only music video.

I had done some production work on the 1983 Country Music Awards, and shortly after that, Dad's agent, Mort Viner, asked me to direct a music video of a song from Dad's new album, *The Nashville Sessions.* Most of the songs on the album were country tunes, but the one that they chose for the video was an uptempo number called "Since I Met You Baby." I was excited about the chance to direct Dad in the video, having seen his movies for so many years and taken all those still photos of him on the show. Plus, this would be his first music video, one of the new entertainment mediums that had emerged in the 1980s.

While I had shot several music videos before, those were all in the controlled environment of a studio. For Dad's video, the plan was to shoot on location at a place called Vasquez Rock near the California coast. Remote, with stunning scenery, it's a very "shoot friendly" place. Or so I thought.

The production number called for Dad to sing the song in this sort of lunar rock landscape, strolling among a bevy of young women we dubbed the "Dean-agers." The young women were all outfitted in black, form-fitting cocktail dresses. They had slicked-back hair, dark sunglasses, and pillbox hats. Later, more than a few people wondered if our Dean-agers had been an inspiration for Robert Palmer's 1986 "Addicted to Love" video.

The plan was that as Dad walked among these women, who were standing in statuesque poses or lying prone in the sandy dirt of the desert, he would swing a golf club, strolling along while singing against this otherworldly backdrop. It was a good plan and I thought we had everything covered.

I'm sure Dad was a little skeptical as Mort drove him out to the location and they found themselves driving and driving and driving. Vasquez Rock is a long way from civilization, and I'm sure Dad was muttering, "What the hell has Rico done here?"

When he arrived, the first thing Dad asked for was a cup of coffee. We had thousands of dollars worth of lighting gear, sound playback equipment, cameras, and honey wagons full of

Return to me. Mom and Dad, together again, about 1982, at Mom's Robert Lane house. (Gina Martin photo)

support staff, but there wasn't a drop of coffee anywhere. And the nearest coffeepot was at a gas station an hour away. Definitely not the first impression I wanted to make with my father, the star. My friend and production assistant Nick Sanelli headed out to fetch some coffee pronto.

We blocked out the shots, had the lighting ready, and began to shoot. Then we discovered the next big problem. The dirt was so soft, the big camera crane dollies were bogging down and unable to track along evenly as Dad strolled through the scenes. It was a constant game of touch and go, the tension getting worse as the temperature climbed. I was getting frantic.

Dad was as cool as ever. The one thing I saw clearly that day was what a consummate professional he was. The way you film a music video is to play back the song over huge speakers as the talent lip syncs to the words while the action is filmed. The talent has to mouth the words to the song perfectly, because no amount of editing can cover up bad lip-synching. If the talent is off, everybody looks like amateurs.

But Dad nailed it every time. He probably learned to lip-sync back in those Martin and Lewis movie days, when he would break into song in a scene. I had always heard from people in movie and TV production, "Your Dad always comes to the set on time, knows his lines and everybody else's." Now I saw how true that was. He followed the old Spencer Tracy adage, "Get on, hit your mark, say your lines, and get off."

In spite of Dad's best efforts, at the end of the day at Vasquez Rock, I still didn't have the shots I needed in the can. Fighting the dollies and the sand all day had been torture, and the video was supposed to be a one-day shoot. Now I had to ask Dad to come back tomorrow because we still didn't have what I was looking for. But instead of the death march in the desert, I decided to punt and use Mom's house at Robert Lane for the second-day location. I promised Dad that all I would need from him the next day would be three hours at Mom's house. He just said, "OK, pallie, what time?"

The next morning, he came on time. I had asked him to wear a tuxedo, rather than the golfing clothes that we had filmed him in the previous day. I plopped him into a big wicker chair opposite the giant clam at Mom's swimming pool and had the Dean-agers, dressed to the nines, all standing side-by-side along the edge of the pool.

We got everything lit and set and then had him sing the entire song sitting in that chair. Near the end of the song, Dad stood up and the camera dollied back. As Dad hit the final chorus, he gestured with his arms, opening them wide, and in the process bumped the Dean-ager closest to him, knocking her in the pool. She knocked the next Dean-ager into the pool, and so on, domino style, as Dad gave a little smile and started walking toward the house, with that classic rolling gait.

As the music faded, the camera by the pool stayed focused

Coffee's coming, Dad, I swear. On the set of the "Since I Met You Baby" video shoot at Vasquez Rock, 1983.

on his back as he walked into Mom's house, through the formal living room, into the big marble foyer, out those two huge wooden doors. Dad continued walking to his waiting car, got in, and was driven away. That was it. I had told him, we just want you walking out at the end, and he knew I had the shot. Another day at the office.

I edited the pool footage with the scenes from the disastrous shoot in the desert, and the video was a smash. "Since I Met You Baby" was the first crossover video from the "easy listening" genre to get airplay on MTV, and it went over well, getting heavy rotation.

I remember screening the final cut for everyone who had gathered at Dad's house on Loma Vista, and the family thought that Dad looked sensational. He came up to me afterward, put his arm around me, and said, "Pallie, you made me look forty again." That was the biggest compliment he could give me.

I was fortunate to work with Dad a few more times, shooting a series of commercials for Family Fitness Center, a chain of

I know I said just one day Dad, but . . .

health spas in Los Angeles. Deana was a trainer for Family Fitness, and we incorporated Deana, Deana's son Mickey, Gina, and Gail's daughters, Cappy and Liza, into the skit with Dad for the commercial. Although Dad had recently signed a multimillion-dollar advertising endorsement deal with AT&T, he agreed to do the Family Fitness Center commercials as a favor to Deana. I produced the whole campaign with a $25,000 budget, and the commercials ran for a long time in the Southern California market.

After selling her house on Robert Lane, Mom moved into a house on Linden Drive, and Dad would eventually buy a house about five blocks east of Mom's place. It was at her house on Linden that many of us kids would gather regularly for dinners with the two of them. At the time, I was living on my 60-foot motor yacht in Marina Del Ray, Gina and Carl had places in Brentwood and Colorado, while Dean-Paul had a condo in Westwood. But in a way, it hearkened back to those nightly dinners at 601, the same kind of togetherness that we all had missed.

Mom even organized a couple of family outings that she

managed to get Dad to join. One summer in the mid-1980s, Gina and Carl were living at the Caribou Ranch near Boulder, Colorado, the beautiful mountain resort that was a popular retreat for many stars. It was owned by their good friends Lucy and Jim Guercio, the producer of the band Chicago. Elton John recorded his *Caribou* album there. Mom decided it would be nice if we all visited Gina and Carl in the mountains.

For transportation, Dad arranged for us to take MGM mogul Kirk Kerkorian's private Boeing 727 jet, a custom-made airliner that was painted stark white, with only the tail numbers distinguishing it. You entered the plane from the rear, up one of those drop-down stairs like notorious hijacker D. B. Cooper parachuted off. Once inside, past the crew quarters, you entered a beautiful salon in the middle of the airplane. It was like walking into the lobby of the MGM Grand in Las Vegas, just sumptuous. There were couches along the sides, and in the middle there was a bar.

Kirk's bedroom was palatial for an airplane, with a huge video screen for movies. The plane had a gourmet kitchen and a flight attendant that waited on our every need. It was one of those experiences that make you think, "Oh, I wish it was farther to Denver." Even Dad, who never liked flying, really enjoyed that flight and the return trip at the end of the weekend. That was the way he liked to do things by then. With as little effort and as much enjoyment as possible.

Maybe buoyed by the success of the Caribou trip, a bit later Mom suggested that Dad go on a boat ride with her and the kids. It sounded painless enough. "For how long?" Dad asked. He thought she answered, "A three-hour cruise." She had actually said three *days*. Wasn't this how *Gilligan's Island* began?

The morning of the cruise, Dad arrived at the dock at Marina Del Rey, where Mom had chartered this immaculate 105-foot motor yacht with captain and crew. He came sauntering down the dock, wearing his usual polo shirt, a windbreaker,

The Family Fitness commercial shoot, with Wayne Tweed and me behind the camera and (left to right) Gail's daughter Cappy, Gina, Gail's daughter Liza, Deana, and Dad.

and khakis. Mom said, "Where's all your stuff?" and Dad answered, "Well, what am I gonna need?"

He still didn't get that this was a three-day voyage, not an afternoon sunning. But Mom dragged him over to Fred Siegel's, a clothing store near the marina, and bought him more clothes. He just played along, sort of amused that Jeanne thought he needed all these shirts and underwear for a boat ride.

The boat got underway and it was a fun time, everyone together on the water, very relaxed. After a couple of hours, Dad started noticing that we had lost sight of land and the boat seemed to be heading out to sea. Finally he asked, "Where is this guy headed?"

"Catalina Island," Mom answered. "We're going to moor for the night at Avalon."

Dad sat bolt upright. "The night?"

"Well, the first night at least. We may move down to the Isthmus for the second or third night."

Dad had been blindsided by this one, but due to his own

fault, and he knew he couldn't complain too loudly. Even though the boat was 105-feet long, there would be no escaping Mom's wrath if he started raising hell about being stuck on a damn boat for three days straight.

Dad wasn't the only one getting antsy. Dean-Paul had things to do, places to go. He was up early the next morning, telling the captain to ease her out of the harbor and head back for Marina Del Rey. Dad, up early as usual, was watching this little mutiny in the making. Officially, he stayed out of the command decision, but on the side, he whispered to Dean-Paul, "OK, pallie, do it."

As the captain began motoring back toward homeport, Mom was enjoying her customary sleeping-in time, enhanced by the hum of the engine and the gentle rocking of the boat. She eventually woke, came up on deck, looked around, and saw no land in sight. Catalina Island was far astern, and she was furious.

Mom and Gina prepare to give Dad a haircut at Mom's house on Robert Lane. (Ricci Martin photo)

A three-hour cruise? No, three days. Dean-Paul's son, Alexander, myself, Dean-Paul, and Dad on the fateful voyage to Catalina in 1983.

Dad was able to deflect blame toward Dean-Paul, but Mom wanted to keelhaul them both when they gleefully jumped ship as soon as the boat nudged into the dock.

The rest of us stayed aboard and headed down toward Malibu for some fishing. The trip didn't work out exactly the way Mom planned. But, for that matter, it didn't work out the way Dad had planned either. Such is the art of compromise.

chapter 9

Dean-Paul

Although I had driven for years before I got a driver's license—whether it was stealthily running a dirtbike up the road to the hills or tugging at the braking-lever reins of our road-ox tank—I got my first street-legal car when I turned 16. It was a switch. I went from a military mastodon devoid of any curved lines to an aerodynamic water droplet of automotive design, with a name that tickled the tongue like one of Dad's Neapolitan melodies, De Tomaso Vallelunga.

The little, no-frills Italian import was a thinly disguised Formula race car, a low-slung fiberglass coupe body bolted onto a racing chassis, with a peppy 4-cylinder Ford Cosworth engine mounted amidships and dwarfed by big Weber carburetors. It was noisy and not that expensive. I admired it from the moment I saw it. Red, of course.

I had the Vallelunga only a few months when Dean-Paul asked to borrow it. His own car had conked out and he needed to get to his helicopter-flying lesson at the Van Nuys airport in Burbank. Given Dean-Paul's infamous reputation with fast cars and solid objects, the news that I had willingly handed over the keys was greeted with amazement and laughter by Alma, our cook. "You let your *brother* drive your new car? Are you crazy?"

But I was confident that Dean-Paul cracking up my prized

Above: Mom going for a ride with Dean-Paul at the controls of a rental helicopter at our ranch near Thousand Oaks, 1970. Right: Dean-Paul Martin. The name alone carries a lot of expectations.

sports car was just too predictable a story line, one of those scenarios that would be so clichéd, we wouldn't even joke about it. Nevertheless, I started to have my first pangs of anxiety when Dean-Paul was an hour overdue. Another hour later, without any sign of my brother or my car, I was running the odds, saying it couldn't happen in a million years. Three hours after his flying lesson ended, he still wasn't home, and by then the entire family was worried.

I will never forget hearing the back door opening and seeing him come into the kitchen as I came down the back stairs, his face spider-webbed with streaks of dried blood. "I got into a wreck with your car," he said slowly, still in shock. "I'm sorry."

I was just glad he was alive. He had obviously been in the worst car wreck of his life, although he was unhurt except for cuts on his face, caused by his own fingernails when he raised his hands at the point of impact. His previous driving mishaps had

been relatively minor bangs and scrapes, nothing too serious—more like notches in the gunbelt. But this crash had shaken him, made all the worse by his guilt that he had smashed up his brother's car.

Dean-Paul had left his flying lesson and decided to take an alternate route from the Valley over to Beverly Hills. Woodland Drive is a back road that leads to Coldwater Canyon. It takes you off the main road through a twisting side canyon dotted by houses, a park, and a fire station. It is not a shortcut. You have to go out of your way to take the side road, and it doesn't save any time, but it provides less traffic and more curves.

Dean-Paul was intimately familiar with high-performance cars and driving, having just recently bought a Ferrari P3 model that had been entered in Le Mans. He had decided to see what my little Vallelunga was made of, so he took Woodland Drive. Working the gears up through the higher revs, Dean-Paul sped around a corner to find a homeowner slowly backing out of a driveway directly in his path.

He swerved and planted the car nose-first into a cement lamp post along the side of the road. The Vallelunga shattered like a Graham cracker. The fuel tank in the front of the car collapsed and absorbed much of the impact, as did the steering column. The four-point racing harness probably saved his life.

Mom told me later that she was so torn that night in her sympathies. In one room, she had a son who had survived a very close call and in another room she had a son whose first car had been totaled by his bigger brother. The next day, when I saw the car, the only thing that was recognizable was the back end. The front had disintegrated. I couldn't believe all Dean-Paul had sustained were some small cuts to his face. He had been incredibly fortunate.

I didn't complain about the loss of my car, but Mom secretly contacted Bob Neal, a friend of hers and a car buff, and he immediately set out to find another De Tomaso Vallelunga to

My 1969 De Tomaso Mangusta. No liquor stores were robbed in the acquisition of this car.

replace my shattered sports car. Easier said than done. Over the few years they were made, there were only fifty Vallelungas produced, and just a handful had ever been imported to the states. Bob persevered, however, locating one in a showroom in Milan, Italy.

Mom was always very frugal when it came to giving money to us kids. She was a strict believer in teaching us the value of a dollar and always worried about spoiling us. Dad, naturally, was the opposite. The saying around our house was always, "You have to go through Mom to get five bucks from Dad." But in this case, Mom must have felt that a loosening of purse strings was in order. Within three weeks after Dean-Paul's wreck, a new red Vallelunga was in the driveway for me, straight off the showroom floor in Italy and delivered via air freight. I'm sure the delivery charges alone were significantly more than the $3,500 price tag of the car.

A few years later, I sold that Vallelunga after I bought its more potent successor, the De Tomaso Mangusta. The person who bought the Vallelunga paid me in cash, and I remember going up to Dad's house and handing him the money from the sale to thank him for replacing the crashed car.

He looked at the big wad of cash with puzzlement. "What, did you rob a liquor store, pallie?" he asked me with a grin.

Dean-Paul apologized for months about the wreck, but I never carried any resentment over the episode. I felt sorrier for him, because I knew how bad he felt and that he was a little humiliated by the whole thing. Dean-Paul always put a lot of pressure on himself to succeed in everything he did.

Perhaps more than any of us kids, Dean-Paul felt the weight of expectations as the son of Dean Martin. The name alone puts you in that zone where you cannot hide. Although Craig was the eldest of Dad's kids, he never had to live up to Dad's image, nor did he care to. It's funny, but as Craig grows older, I find he has more and more of Dad's mannerisms.

Dean-Paul was never told that he had to live up to the name, but I think that was always playing in the back of his mind. The pattern seemed to be set even as a young teen, when he broke into the music business with Dino, Desi, and Billy. He had a taste of that life early on with their rapid rise to success, but I never got the impression he was too crestfallen when the band broke up. He had taken to wearing a gold wedding band on his left hand while on tour, as much to fend off advances from girls as to try to appear older than he was.

But the name was there. Through most of his childhood, he was always "Dino" or "Dino Jr." In his music days and his early acting career, he was generally billed as "Dino Martin Jr." But I remember when he got older, just turning 20 and getting serious about acting, he asked everyone in the family to please start calling him "Dean-Paul." Of course, the household was razzing him: "You'll always be Dino" and "What's this Dean *hyphen* Paul stuff?"

He was always "Dino" to Mom.

Mom and Grandma Peggy ignored the request and continued to call him Dino, while Dad merely said, "OK, pallie, that's fine with me." I figured he deserved that respect and from that point on, I would refer to him as Dean-Paul and would address him in person as Dean. In time, it sunk in with everyone in the family and it became odd to call him Dino.

No doubt part of the reason for his desire to be known as "Dean-Paul" Martin was to separate himself a bit from Dad. Although it works for you at times, the jealousy involved in being the child of a huge celebrity can be a major detriment in pursuing a career. People dislike you before they've even met you, because of a preconceived notion of what you must be like, a perception based on kid stars that probably deserved the derision. The baggage arrives before you do. I've had more than one person tell me, "Hey, you're a good guy after all," at the close of our first meeting. They had been expecting one thing and then

Dad, Dean-Paul, and Mom, about 1952. (Gerald K. Smith photo)

were a bit surprised when they discovered the stereotype didn't hold up.

When your name is the same as your famous father's, there is little you can do to counter those opinions. I remember one summer Dean-Paul was playing a tennis tournament in Ojai, north of Ventura. After the match, he walked to where his Lamborghini Mura was parked and found that the windshield had been broken, the mirrors snapped off, and a screwdriver had been jammed through the hood. Someone had just trashed his car because he was Dean Martin's son.

Because of his name, I think Dean-Paul always felt he had to be an over-achiever. It was nothing that Mom or Dad expected of him; it was something he demanded of himself. He wanted to make sure people knew the things that he accomplished were deserved on his own merit, that he hadn't just been handed something on a silver platter.

So he would go into something full bore, trying to cut his own swath. He began studying to be a doctor and started working at Martin Luther King Hospital, which on some nights was hell with the lid off. People came in from gang fights in South Central with knife wounds, gunshots, every manner of violent injury you could imagine. Since Dad avoided hospitals and doctors, it was certainly a new career path in the Martin household.

Dean-Paul was always physically adept at sports, and when he would start to play a sport he would get very serious about it, almost single-minded. That intense focus would last until he became disillusioned by the realities of reaching the very peak of a sport or profession, since if he was going to do something, he wanted to be one of the best. Football was like that. He became fixated on playing professional football and was drafted by a short-lived pro team called the Las Vegas Casinos. But when he saw how players were forced to abuse their bodies through chemical boosters, he decided that it wasn't for him and he gravitated toward tennis.

On the tennis court, he was very serious, and it paid off, with his play getting him nationally ranked. He was ruthlessly competitive, and played frequently with Spencer Segura, the son of tennis great Pancho Segura. At times, our tennis court seemed like a legends tennis tournament, with people like Rod Laver, Arthur Ashe, Jimmy Connors, Pancho Gonzales, and Chris Evert all taking their turn at the net.

Tennis was a natural outgrowth of Mom's parties, and in the early days, she and Dad were a fairly formidable doubles team. One of my favorite people and a fantastic man to watch play tennis was football great Jim Brown, a huge guy who was unbelievably fast on the court. In spite of his tough character image, he

On the court, Dean-Paul was strictly business, earning him national ranking.

was always warm and approachable around me, supportive in no small part I think because of the friendship he saw I had with Wayne Tweed.

While Dean-Paul was good enough to play on the professional circuit, he saw the level of commitment and isolation required to reach the point where you were among the top players in the world, and he decided that wasn't for him. The tennis racquets went into the closet, although his skill did help him land a role in the 1979 movie *Players*.

He had a passion for flying since he was a boy. Machine-gun escapades aside, gravity was the one law he had trouble obeying. Whether it was jumping motorcycles, racing cars, or flying planes, Dean-Paul's love affair with locomotion always seemed to be conducted at the edge of maximum performance. He knew his limits and he seldom did anything stupid. Instead, his accidents were usually due to the actions of another. He would be put in a situation from which he would narrowly escape, walking away from the wreckage once again to tell the story.

Dean-Paul learned to fly in his teens, starting with small, single-engine planes, then graduating to a helicopter, one of those old Bells with the bubble-shaped canopy that he flew around the ranch in Thousand Oaks. He had always wanted to fly jets, and eventually he joined the U.S. Air Force, making the grade to enroll in Air Training Command in Mississippi.

Once he was immersed in flight school, he began to see what a long haul it would be as a career military pilot. He also had married figure skater Dorothy Hamill, "America's Sweetheart," after his divorce from Olivia Hussey, and he wasn't looking forward to possible duty stations out of Southern California or overseas.

At the same time, he won the lead in a new NBC teen-oriented adventure series, *The Misfits of Science*, about a group of young crime-fighters with superhuman abilities. As Dr. Billy

Mom with Dean-Paul and fiancée, figure skater Dorothy Hamill. Dean-Paul was graduating Air Training Command in Columbus, Mississippi.

Hayes, he starred opposite Courteney Cox, who would go on to fame as Monica in the hit comedy series *Friends*.

The series was a huge break for Dean-Paul, but he didn't want to give up his chance to fly jets with Uncle Sam picking up the gas tab. So he opted for the Air National Guard, which stationed him at March Air Force Base near Riverside, California. Although he had one typical Dean-Paul close-call—he once careened off the runway while landing at Redlands Field during a heavy crosswind and destroyed the landing gear of his jet, yet walked away unscathed—he was considered a top-notch pilot by his peers. He quickly made the rank of captain in the Air National Guard, flying F-4C Phantom jets.

At the time, it seemed he had found his niche after diving head-first into so many other pursuits. His acting career was taking off and the Air Guard provided him that adrenaline rush he craved, while still giving him flexibility to pursue acting jobs.

One Saturday morning, he took his 14-year-old son to March Air Force Base so Alexander could watch Dean-Paul's squadron take off for a low-level bombing practice run they were scheduled to fly that day. It was March 21, 1987, and the weather was nasty for the spring, the sky spitting snow as a storm front rolled in from the coast and over the San Bernadino Mountains. The strong winds played such havoc that jets were forced to take off from the opposite end of the runway—something that can disorient a pilot from the start.

Alexander watched Dean-Paul's Phantom screech into the

The wild blue yonder awaits. Dean-Paul, about 1986 at March Air Force Base.

dark sky. The squadron had been cleared for a "maximum climb" takeoff, powering straight up into the scattered cloud cover 4,700 feet above. Alexander waited at the base while the squadron conducted the training exercise. After a time, the jets in Dean-Paul's squadron materialized out of the blackness and started touching down, one right after the other. After the third ship landed, there was a long wait. The fourth jet, with Dean-Paul and his backseat weapons operator, Ramon Ortiz, was missing. It had disappeared from radar nine minutes after takeoff.

The military had few details. The other pilots were unsure where they had become separated from their flight leader, and there had been no distress call radioed in. The emergency transponder on Dean-Paul's jet—designed to go off in a crash and provide a homing beacon to rescuers—had not been triggered, nor had the transponders each airman wore.

Upon hearing Dean-Paul's plane was missing, a small group gathered at Mom's house on Linden in Beverly Hills—Dad, Mom, Alexander, my sister Gina, Carl Wilson, myself, and Scott Sandler, Dean-Paul's closest friend. By now, the disappearance of Dean-Paul's aircraft had become a national story. The Los Angeles radio and television stations were leading every newscast with search updates.

The next day, the military still had no clues as to Dean-Paul's whereabouts. They had spotted no crash debris and still had not located the transponder signals. We were told that Dean-Paul and his crewman had ample survival gear and knew how to use it. Plus, we all knew Dean-Paul and his uncanny ability to dodge the bullet. I kept thinking of that day, when he had come home from crashing my car, shaken but alive. Every phone call, every knock at the door, I kept expecting it to be Dean-Paul.

The third day came and still no word. It was as if Dean-Paul's jet had simply vanished from the sky. The area where radar contact had been lost was not some desolate wilderness, but instead the populated foothills of the San Bernadino Range.

Someone had to have seen or heard something. Waiting and wondering, discussing all the possible scenarios, fielding phone calls from well-wishers—it all began to wear on us.

Dad was getting especially morose, staring blankly out the window, seldom talking, and a cigarette always in his hand. He was the barometer of the family's mood, and I tried to coax some encouragement from him, but his frustration, feeling helpless to find his son, was overwhelming.

"You know, pallie," he said to me one afternoon, "all the money I have, all the money in the world, and I can't do a damn thing to find him."

By the fourth day, we were living in a nightmare. Each ring of the phone brought hope that there was some news, any news, but invariably it was someone calling to check on us or to see if there was any word. I started answering the phone with an irritation in my voice. Even when a woman on the other end of the line said, "This is the White House calling. The President would like to speak to Mr. Martin please," I brusquely said, "Tell him to hold on."

Dad got on the line with President Ronald Reagan, and the two talked quietly for several minutes. Ronnie had found Dad simpatico in many respects; they were both easygoing, had done a lot of westerns, and had mastered the art of self-deprecating humor. They were friends, and Ronnie told Dad he had ordered an SR-71 spy plane to overfly the search area and photograph the region. They were doing everything they could to find Dean-Paul's plane, he told Dad. The Reagan family's prayers were with us for Dean-Paul's safe return, but the pain in Ronnie's voice was as much for Dean-Paul as it was for Dad. I think he knew that family was one of the few things Dad truly cherished and now his son had been taken from him. President Reagan consoled Dad as best he could, but the reality that Dean-Paul was probably dead was unavoidable.

I think Dad realized then he had lost his son, but even in

that desperate, horrible moment he kept his dignity. In a calm voice filled with reverence and honor, he told Ronald Reagan: "Thank you, my president." He then turned to Mom and said, "Jeanne, Nancy wants to talk to you." Handing her the phone, he walked into another room to be alone.

By that afternoon, our nerves were frayed from not knowing anything about Dean-Paul's whereabouts, made worse by the growing likelihood that with each passing hour he was probably gone. In desperation, I suggested we talk to a psychic. Scott and I grabbed one of Dean-Paul's flight suits and went to the home of Peter Hurkos, a prominent Los Angeles psychic who had accompanied Roman Polanski when he went to the house on Cielo Drive for the first time after Sharon Tate had been murdered there by the Manson family. We had been told that Hurkos could help us locate Dean-Paul. For $5,000 cash, of course.

The moment I walked into Hurkos's home, I was uncomfortable. The room was dark, and the walls were covered with eerie paintings and photographs. With little fanfare, Hurkos took the cash, touched the flight suit, and started trembling, almost convulsing.

"They're both dead," he croaked. "They're both dead and they went in fast. Look at my hands!" He was quivering almost uncontrollably, seemingly shocked by whatever paranormal vibe he was receiving from the flight suit.

This was not what I wanted to hear, nor the way I thought these people worked. Hurkos vaguely gestured to a map where they were, but neither Scott nor I were paying much attention.

He went on to other things that he saw, asking me whether I was going to move because he saw fire in my future. While it was odd at the time, it stuck with me and I decided to put a smoke alarm on the boat where I lived. Months later, while I was in the shower in the rear stateroom of the boat, a forced-air heater mounted above the berth seized up and began to smolder.

Doing what he loved. Dean-Paul, in 1986, preparing to board his Air Force T-38 jet. (Guy Webster photo)

The smoke alarm went off, which got me out of the shower in time to shut off the heater just before it burst into flames. Any later and I would have been trapped. I attribute Hurkos's premonition with saving my life.

But that day at his house, my mind was on Dean-Paul and I wasn't sure if Hurkos was helping. Scott and I left and went back to Mom's house.

Everyone was on edge waiting to hear what the psychic had said and I dreaded telling them. "Hurkos said they're dead," I announced. "Maybe we should get a second opinion."

Mom had spoken with Shirley MacLaine earlier and Shirley suggested we try a friend of hers, Char Margolis, who was a "psychic intuitive," a person who allegedly could make contact with departed spirits. After the bizarre experience with Peter Hurkos, I was worried this might be a repeat performance, but we agreed to give it a try. At least it felt good to be doing something rather than sitting in the house all day, waiting for news. Scott called Char and she agreed to meet us the next day at the Beverly Hills home where she was staying.

Char was a small woman, but she impressed me right away. Instead of just touching one of Dean-Paul's flight suits, she wanted to go to March Air Force Base and talk with the airmen who knew Dean-Paul. It was worth a try, but thus far the military had been treating Dean-Paul's disappearance as a closed-door affair with no outside interference. Scott, Char, and I drove out to the base and, to my surprise, the military officials in charge actually agreed to allow Char to talk with searchers and Dean-Paul's squadron members. One of the officers later told us that psychics were periodically consulted in searches for downed pilots, but the Air Force preferred to keep that particular branch of military intelligence quiet.

Opposite: Father and son, 1954. Dad escorting Dean-Paul to his third birthday party at 601 Mountain.

Char spread out a big map of the search area on a floor and started talking to the airmen, flight mechanics, and officers about Dean-Paul and Ramon, his "wizzo"—military slang for weapons operator. It was an odd scene. Here was this petite woman in blue jeans surrounded by military brass and men in flight suits, all of them looking at her with more than a little skepticism.

The conversations rambled, and Char was running her fingers over the map when she glanced up and suddenly gasped. "This room is just filled with spirits of dead pilots," she told me, claiming she saw images of fliers dating back to World War I who were wanting to help her find the crash site of Dean-Paul's jet.

Char kept coming back to a spot on the map near the Little San Gorgonio Mountains, a small range on the lip of the San Bernadinos, clustered near Mount San Gorgonio. The sector had been repeatedly searched, but Char was convinced Dean-Paul's plane was there. When the searchers protested that they had looked there many times and found nothing, she said, "No, I believe it's right in this area, maybe hidden by a tree with something hanging from the branches." The officers leading the search were reluctant but agreed to have the pilots concentrate once again on that spot she was convinced held the wreckage of the missing plane.

We wanted to go along, but the military didn't want civilians aboard search aircraft. One officer said we were free to inspect the area on our own, since it was civilian airspace, and an Air Force captain who knew Dean-Paul volunteered to help us. So we drove to the Riverside airport and chartered a helicopter.

Throughout all of her questioning and divining about Dean-Paul, Char had never mentioned whether she believed he was dead, although I think she knew. And I suppose I did too. I remember lifting off in that helicopter—Char, Scott, and me in the back seat, the pilot and Air Force captain up front—thinking how Dean-Paul must be looking down from heaven, having a pretty good laugh. Here I was with a pyschic, his best friend, in a chartered helicopter, flying around trying to find him.

Even though Char had never been over the area, she seemed to be familiar with the terrain, giving the helicopter pilot directions just as the Air Force captain did. As we neared the site that Char had pinpointed, the pilot suddenly announced that we had to turn back. The military had located the crash site, cordoned off the airspace, and was ordering all civilian craft out of the area. The wreckage of Dean-Paul's plane had been found in the precise spot where Char had said it would be.

There was no word on survivors, but as we were heading back, we were told by the Air Force that we had permission to land our helicopter at March Air Force Base, which rarely allowed civilian aircraft to land. The extraordinary clearance meant that the Air Force knew, from the destruction at the crash site, that Dean-Paul was dead. Allowing his family to land their helicopter at the base was the least they could do for a fallen pilot. I also suspect there were a lot of people at the base who had a newfound respect for Char's intuitive abilities.

No one said much back at the base, but it was clear they knew Dean-Paul and Ramon Ortiz were gone. Walking away from the helicopter, I had a sense of relief that we had found him, coupled with an intense sorrow that my big brother had indeed been killed.

I drove Char home and thanked her profusely for helping end the uncertainty that had plagued my family during the ordeal. She never got the credit she deserved in finding my brother; it's not as if the military was going to acknowledge her role. I certainly do.

I went back to Mom's house and met with the rest of the family to wait for the official word. That evening, we were told that a colonel from the base was coming to the house. I took aside Alexander, Dean-Paul's son, and told him this was probably going to be bad news. He had seen his father fly off five days earlier and now I had to tell him that Dean-Paul probably was gone.

The colonel said that Dean-Paul and Ramon had died instantly when their Phantom plowed into the side of a canyon wall. The impact was so great that the huge Phantom, whose jet turbines were the size of a Volkswagen bus, had been reduced to pieces no larger than a basketball. Of Dean-Paul Martin and Ramon Ortiz, there was nothing left bigger than a fingernail, save for what was in their helmets.

Apparently, Dean-Paul had taken emergency maneuvers to avoid Mount San Gorgonio as the squadron was crossing the mountain range in blizzard conditions. The military had a 500-foot window of airspace over the mountaintop, and to fly higher, the Air Guard needed permission to enter commercial airspace from the control tower at Ontario International Airport.

We would learn later from the subsequent investigation that as Dean-Paul was approaching the mountain, he requested "altitude immediately" from Ontario to safely clear the peak in the wildly buffeting winds. His radio had been "red-tagged" for inspection, because of previous intermittent problems. The tower, dealing with civilian air traffic problems due to the storm, told the Phantoms to standby. Dean-Paul repeated his request to increase altitude but the reply again was to stand by.

By now, the mountaintop was dead ahead and the other members of the squadron gave up waiting for permission and yanked back their control sticks, figuring they would take their chances with a possible jetliner above rather than a definite mountainside ahead.

Some time later, after I had listened to the tapes of the radio communications between Dean-Paul and Ontario control, I was contacted by my friend Bob Carey, who found out the air traffic controller on duty had instantly realized she had waited too long to clear the Phantoms into commercial airspace. She was so overcome with grief that she had to be carried out of the control tower. I told him to please get word to her that she should not blame herself and that I did not consider her responsible for Dean-Paul's death.

The investigation showed Dean-Paul had attempted to turn sharply away from the onrushing peak rather than violate commercial airspace and increase altitude. In a way, that was classic Dean-Paul. He was trying to find a way to use all the thrust he could, never showing any fear by pushing the plane to its limit in a maximum-G turn to avoid the mountain ahead and the potential for civilian casualties above.

When he hard-sticked the Phantom left, the plane lost altitude from the turn. Dean-Paul kicked in the afterburners to give the jet power to compensate for the loss of elevation, pushing the Phantom through a supersonic about-face from Mount San Gorgonio, the highest peak in southern California at 11,499 feet.

The turn was tight enough but not high enough. The jet was too low, and as it completed the 180-degree maneuver away from the face of the peak, it slammed into a granite canyon wall in the nearby Little San Gorgonio Mountains in a deafening fireball that was swallowed up by the raging thunderstorm. An investigation later estimated the plane was traveling inverted at 560 mph at an altitude of 5,500 feet when it made impact.

This time, there was no great escape.

Dean-Paul's funeral was at Veterans Memorial in Westwood, only a few days after Mom's birthday. The Air Force asked if we wanted "Taps" to be played at Dean-Paul's graveside, and, for my part, I said no, thinking that hearing the mournful bugle farewell would be too much for all of us to bare. The Air Guard instead offered to do a "missing man" formation flyover, which we agreed to. It was highly unusual to allow a low-level pass of military jets over a populated area like Westwood, but the FAA approved the request.

Gone, but not forgotten. Dean-Paul died in 1987 at age 35.

I had forgotten about the flyover on the day of the funeral until that moment, perfectly timed at the close of the graveside service, when I heard the fast-approaching thunder of the jets. They rocketed overhead in a diamond formation, and as they flew by, one jet broke off to the left, the lone white contrail in its wake arcing across the empty blue sky, signifying the missing flier.

As I heard those shrieking turbofans, I realized I had been wrong about "Taps." The sound of those jet engines was more heart wrenching than any musical note I have ever heard.

It was at that moment I realized, "Oh my God, he's gone." He was my brother and my closest friend. We had never raised a hand toward each other in anger, and sibling rivalry was never part of our vocabulary. We had a closeness that was such a regular part of our family for so long that, at that moment, I wondered how we would go on without him.

It was over. Dean-Paul was gone and our family would never be the same.

chapter 16

Whaddya Say, Pallie?

The day of Dean-Paul's funeral, a thin, dark-haired man quietly slipped in and sat in the back. When the service was over, he discreetly left.

We would have never known, but someone mentioned to Dad how nice it was to see Jerry at the funeral. Dad was astonished to discover Jerry Lewis had come to the service, not so much because Dad didn't expect Jerry to come, but because Jerry had a way of always attracting attention to himself.

While the bitter feelings had mellowed since the breakup some thirty years earlier, the two men had seldom spoken or seen each other. Frank had first reunited them during one of Jerry's muscular dystrophy telethons in 1976, but there was always a distance between them.

Something about Jerry's quiet sympathy at Dean-Paul's funeral touched Dad. A short time later, Dad called Jerry to thank him for coming and just to talk. They spoke on the phone for a long time, and Dad later told me that at the end of the conversation, they expressed their love for each other.

From that point on, it seemed like things were set right between them and they maintained regular contact. If anything good came out of Dean-Paul's death, it was that Martin and Lewis finally made their peace. Yet Dean-Paul's death in 1987 at age 35 was the beginning of a downward spiral in Dad's health and enthusiasm for life.

One of the single most traumatic events for a parent is the death of a child. To lose a child, it's been said, is to lose a piece of yourself. That was equally true for Dad and for Mom. They had each other to share their grief, but neither of them would be one to discuss such feelings of anguish openly. In spite of living very public lives, they were intensely private people when it came to mourning the loss of their son.

We resumed our regular gatherings every week or so at Mom's house: Mom, Dad, myself, Gina, and sometimes Craig, Claudia, Gail, Deana, and Dean-Paul's son, Alexander. Dad would come over—his house on North Maple was just about five blocks from Mom's place—and I would mix him his usual "orangey" screwdriver, and then he would taper into a nice scotch and soda.

He liked to sit in front of the television to eat, even at Mom's house, and Jay Judson, our childhood friend from 601 who became an accomplished chef and worked for Mom for many years, would serve Dad his favorite broiled garlic chicken at the coffee table in front of the TV.

Gina was married to Carl Wilson late in 1987, a celebration which helped raise everyone's spirits after the sadness earlier in the year. She and Carl had dated for seven years. After Carl and Annie Hinsche (Billy's sister) had divorced, Carl told me he had a crush on Gina and I suggested he come to a gig my band was playing at Madame Wong's in West L.A., since Gina would be there. The two of them spent much of the night talking in the booth, which was the beginning of their relationship.

The ensuing courtship was a little lengthy, as far as Mom was concerned. She would periodically press Gina with the proverbial, "When are you guys going to get married?" noting that the two of them basically lived together and Gina accompanied Carl on the road with the Beach Boys tours. Gina would gently ask her not to rock the boat. But during dinner one evening at her house, Mom popped the question to Carl as to when he was going to marry Gina.

Carl grinned with a little embarrassment, while I believe Gina was furious. She later told Mom that Carl was indeed about to ask her, but now Mom's teasing had made any proposal appear as if it was prompted by her asking.

Carl never did anything he didn't want to do, and one thing he had wanted to do since he and Gina fell in love was marry my sister. In a short time, the two were engaged, and their wedding at the MGM Grand in Las Vegas was a beautiful event, a nice glimmer of sunshine in what had been a gray season for our family.

There were still clouds, of course. Our beloved grandmother Peggy, Mom's mother, died in April 1989 at the age of 86. She had lived with us through all those years at 601 and was dear to each of us. Her passing added another weight to Mom and Dad's hearts.

Perhaps hoping to lighten things up, Mom booked us all on a passage to London aboard the *QE2* ocean liner. We each had beautiful staterooms on board, with balconies that overlooked the ocean, and the service was first-class. But Dad clearly did not want to be there. His mood was uncharacteristically sullen. This was no day cruise to Avalon, it was a transatlantic voyage, and there would be no turning around, no Dean-Paul to lead the mutiny. One night in the crowded dining room, the tension between Dad and Mom boiled over. She said something that irritated him and he slammed his fist down onto our table, rattling the china and silencing the room full of diners. "I'm never right," he said. Later, Mom told me if she had the chance, she would have pushed him overboard.

It was very unlike Dad to do that, but it was one of those situations where he had obviously agreed to go on a trip that he really had not wanted to take. He was always noncombative. You didn't want to ask Dad to do something because he would likely say yes, even though he didn't really want to do it. That was one of the keys to Dad: don't ask him to do something. Frank had a saying, "Don't tell me—suggest." Although Dad would never say it, the variation for him was, "Don't ask me—just offer."

Annie Rasmussen, my wife, always said I should invite Dad to our house. But I would never do that because then he would be put in a position where he felt he couldn't say no. Instead, I'd say, "Dad, you know if you ever want to, you're welcome to come on up to the house." He was fine with that, because he didn't feel any pressure that he had to come over.

That aspect of his personality came into play with the "Legends" concert tour of 1989, when Frank decided that he, Dad, and Sammy Davis Jr. should reunite for a series of concerts at big arenas around the country. Dad was in favor of the original plan—the three of them would do the tour via train, travelling to major cities by rail. Dad loved trains, and the idea of his own private car, with a limo to take him to the show and back to the train, appealed to him.

But, he later told me, "As it got closer, everyone loused it up." To keep the schedule tight, the train was scrapped in favor of flying, and suddenly, it turned into another maniac thing with airports and baggage and hotel rooms, all the things he hated. He was supposed to be retired. But now, he had agreed to do the show with Frank—who saw the concert tour as a way to counteract Dad's increasing distance since Dean-Paul's death. Once again, Dad had gotten roped into doing something that he really didn't want to do.

But Frank thought the tour would be good for Dad. It was ironic that the mountain peak Dean-Paul had swerved to avoid, Mount San Gorgonio, had a decade earlier claimed the life of Frank's 82-year-old mother, Natalie "Dolly" Sinatra, in a plane crash. She and three others were killed when their Gates Learjet took off from Palm Springs on January 6, 1977, on their way to see Frank's opening-night show at Caesar's Palace in Las Vegas.

The cause of that crash also was confusion over the flight clearance given to the pilot by an air traffic controller shortly

In the end, Jerry and Dad made their peace.

after takeoff, with the plane failing to turn and instead crashing into the mountain. Frank had gone on stage knowing his mother's plane was missing, and the search took three long days. Dad had been a pallbearer at her funeral. Frank, for all his bombastic ways, perhaps understood more than anyone what our family had gone through, and he was there for Dad in one of his darkest hours.

Still, Dad was reluctant to do the tour. It was difficult transferring their intimate Vegas showroom act to venues that seated crowds for hockey and basketball games. Dad was a crooner, and while he and Frank certainly sang well together, his style was not one to boom out over a big orchestra and fill up an arena like Ethel Merman belting out the "Star Spangled Banner." Singing in an arena, he was out of his element.

Adding to Dad's aggravation was Frank's well-meaning attempts to turn back the clock to the Rat Pack routine. After the show in Chicago, Frank was in the hotel bar with his cronies, revving up for a long night, demanding to know were Dean was. Dad, of course, was up in his hotel room in bed.

So Frank began phoning Dad's room, yelling, "Dago, get your ass down here to the bar! What are you doing in bed?" In the old days, Dad could have begged off with the line about having a woman upstairs, but they were both too old to fall for that. He told Frank he was tired and was going to bed."You get down here, Dag, or I'll come up there and set your bed on fire!" Frank yelled over the phone. And Dad knew Frank was crazy enough to do just that.

It was the last straw. I always pictured in my mind how furious Dad must have been as he got dressed to go down to the bar to render unto Frank what was Frank's. Afterward, Dad told his agent Mort Viner, "It's over. I want to go home." Mort prepared a press release that said Dad had a kidney problem and needed to see his doctor in Los Angeles. Late that night, Dad flew home aboard a chartered plane. He even went to the hospital for the full effect.

He walked away from Frank, never telling him why. He loved Frank and he wasn't vengeful; he never wanted to do anything to hurt him. But he just couldn't endure Frank's routine anymore. Liza Minelli agreed to substitute for Dad for the rest of the tour, which was renamed "The Ultimate Event."

Sadly, it was Sammy Davis Jr. who probably should have quit the tour and checked into a hospital. Although Sammy never mentioned his illness or showed any signs of pain during the shows, he was hospitalized with throat cancer after the reunion tour ended.

Dad went to see Sammy on his death bed at Cedars Sinai, an indication of how special Sammy was to Dad, a man who detested hospitals. Sammy was a sweetheart, someone who was as meek as Frank was wild. The two of them had monkeyed through the Vegas years and on into the *Cannonball Run* movies, and when Sammy died from cancer on May 16, 1990, another part of Dad died, too.

For me, a new part of my life was just beginning. On a

Our grandmother Peggy, 1983.

flight with Mom to Gina and Carl's new house in Colorado, I noticed a cute blonde flight attendant working the first-class cabin. She noticed me looking at her and gave me a big smile. I immediately thought to myself, "Oh, I'm in."

Getting rhythm from a flight attendant was not something I had experienced before. I got up to go forward to the lavatory, and I introduced myself to her. She told me her name was Annie. Then I noticed an "Out of Order" sign on the lavatory and I asked, "Is it working?"

"I don't know," she said. "Give it a try."

Despite the sign on the door, the lavatory worked, and I wanted to do something clever on my exit to keep up the conversation. Grabbing one of the small wrapped soaps from the sink, I walked into the aisle. Annie was still there. Holding up the bar of soap, I told Annie, "the lav is working fine, but these little mints taste soapy." She laughed and we hit it off from there.

A couple of weeks later, on one of her layovers in L.A., we met in a bar before going out to dinner. The waiter came up to take our drink order, and I said, "I'll have a screwdriver with a vodka sidecar." He turned to Annie, who said, "I'll have a double kamikaze with nuked warm gin back." Right then, I knew this was the girl for me.

We were married July 20, 1991, at poolside at Mom's house

on Linden Drive, and it was a memorable evening. It was also the last time the entire Martin family would be together.

Although Dad was booked into a few more Las Vegas shows, he eventually lost any desire to perform. Shortly after Annie and I had married, we were living at Lake Arrowhead and wanted to go see his show in Las Vegas. We were getting ready to leave when I got a phone call informing me that Dad had cancelled his performance. He never went back to the stage. He just didn't care anymore.

Dad had gotten into a routine by now, with trips to the local restaurants taking the place of his daily golf game. Golf had been Dad's way of relaxing and exercising. I never knew how he was introduced to the game—there weren't many golf courses in Steubenville when he was growing up—but I suspect it was the result of having daylight hours to kill in Las Vegas or through celebrity pro-am tournaments. During all those years as I grew up, golf would be the way he liked to spend his spare time. And it was his time. None of us boys ever went golfing with him.

When his back injury became so bad that he simply could not swing a club, Dad lost another thing that was dear to him. He was no longer outside, walking the course, breathing the fresh air, and getting exercise. For a while, he had a rowing machine at his home that he used regularly, but he soon tired of that monotony. So he would sit at home alone, watching westerns, and make the daily sojourn to the little restaurants that would become his legendary haunts for the last years of his life.

By now, Dad had moved to his small house on Maple Drive. His place was not fancy, just a little living room where he had a pool table and a nice couch and television, a small dining room and kitchen, then his study, bedroom, and bathroom. The walls were covered with all of his gold and platinum albums, some two dozen, and many of the movie posters, mostly the westerns. Outside, there was no backyard to speak of, just a small swimming pool next to the side of a mountain.

It was all very cozy, close-in. But Dad always liked that. Even though he had claustrophobia, he liked a small living space. He didn't like to walk too far to get from one end of the house to the other. Plus, with the exception of family, he never entertained at his house. It was just him, his guards—off-duty Los Angeles police officers who were more friends than guards—and his cook, Connie. Instead of inviting people to his house, he would meet them at the restaurant La Famiglia. Most Sundays, when La Famiglia was closed, he could be found at the Hamburger Hamlet on Sunset and Doheny.

Dad would also spend a Sunday afternoon or two a month at Mom's house. It was at her house on Linden that we all would celebrate holidays and have Sunday dinners, much like the old times at 601.

For Christmas in 1993, we all gathered at Mom's house for dinner. By now, Annie and I were living near Park City, Utah, and had just had our first daughter, Pepper Jazz. Pepper was a little over a year old, and she had been hitting Mom's appetizer tray pretty hard, downing a lot of shrimp and caviar. Even at that age, she had the Martin taste.

Oliver Stone, the movie director, had wanted to meet Dad, so Mom had invited him over to our little Christmas party. I greeted him at the door and led him into the living room. Pepper wandered up, and I introduced Oliver to my daughter. As he picked her up to give her a hug, the appetizers caught up with her fledgling digestive system. Pepper threw up all over Oliver Stone.

He was as gracious as could be, wiping away the regurgitated remnants of the shrimp and caviar platter from his shirt as he ambled around the end of the couch, stuck out his hand, and said, "Hi, Dean!" They had a nice conversation, and Oliver seemed thrilled to meet Dad. Dad had known several of the big directors in Hollywood, masters like Howard Hawks, who had directed *Rio Bravo*. Still, I don't think Dad realized exactly who

It's Frank's world; we're just living in it.

Oliver Stone was and what a tremendous power he was in Hollywood at that time. I was half-expecting Dad to ask, "So, pallie, what westerns have you made?"

It always impressed me how many younger stars paid such honor to Dad, similar to the way superstar athletes seem to melt in the presence of Muhammad Ali. I witnessed several encounters when contemporary stars met Dad in his later years, especially during his dinners at La Famiglia and Da Vinci's. Dad was genuinely flattered when stars like Eddie Murphy or Jay Leno were kind enough to stop by his table and say hello. Dad felt very comfortable at La Famiglia, and truly, everyone there became like a family to him and to us. I would try to visit him regularly, and we would all go to dinner, Dad, Mom, myself, Annie, and Pepper, always seated at his regular table. We went frequently enough that we ended up buying one of those little clip-on child's seats that fit over the edge of the table and just leaving it at the restaurant to use each time we came in.

But the place suffered a blow when an ordinance banning

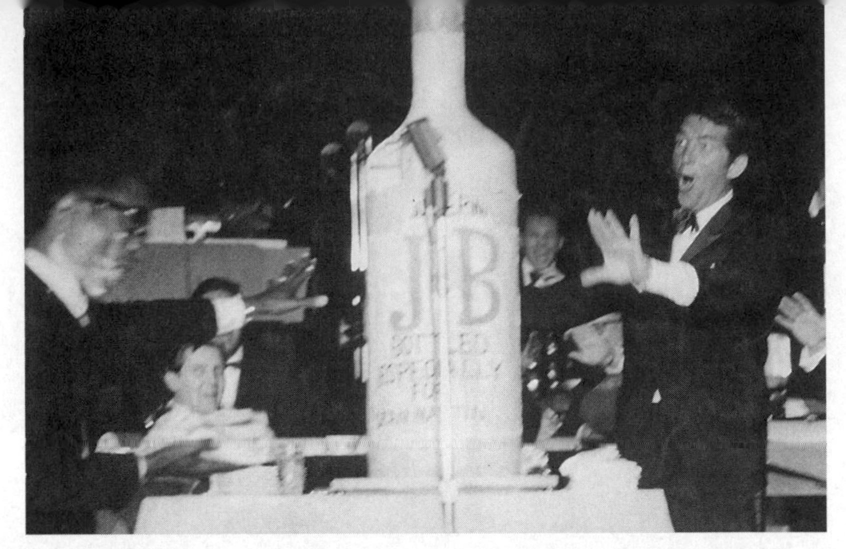

Sammy and Dad, exchanging cake recipes on the stage of the Sands.

smoking in Beverly Hills restaurants was passed. La Famiglia was a cozy, dark little place frequented by an older clientele, people like Dad who were smokers. That was very tough for Dad, not being able to sit in his booth at La Famiglia and smoke.

At the same time, downtown Beverly Hills was changing, getting more ritzy with fancier, trendier restaurants displacing a lot of the old hangouts. One evening, Joe Patti, the owner of La Famiglia and a person whom we viewed as a member of the family, took me back into the kitchen to tell me that business was not good and he doubted he could keep the doors open for long. At the same time, Joe knew Dad needed a place to go every evening, and he hated to take away one of the few things in life Dad looked forward to each day. He had tried to break the news to Dad, but Dad offered to subsidize the restaurant to keep it open. Joe appreciated the offer, but as a restaurateur, he knew he had to get out and do something somewhere else.

Joe hung on for a while longer as Dad's health declined, but there came a point where Joe realized he had to close the doors of La Famiglia at the end of the month. I was visiting in Los Angeles at the time and decided to stop by the restaurant to pick up Pepper's little child seat we had left there for those dinners with Dad.

It was a simple errand, but I dreaded going to the restaurant. All of the people at the restaurant knew that Dad was fading in health, and now, one of the landmarks of the good old days of Beverly Hills was closing down. As I picked up the little chair, I shook hands and hugged the waiters, cooks, and Joe, who had filled a void in Dad's life. When I left, we knew we probably wouldn't see each other again. It was a very sad and emotional moment for us all. Another part of Dad's shrinking world had just slipped away.

He would start frequenting another local restaurant, La Dolce Vita, although it never had the same comfortable feeling that characterized La Famiglia. On Sundays, it was still the Hamlet, where Dad's table near the bar had a good view of the television. They loved him at the Hamlet, and it was there many times that he and I would sit talking about whatever memory came to mind.

Dad was becoming frailer, and he had a tough time getting around. By now, his deteriorating condition was regular fare in the tabloids, and it wasn't unusual for the family to come out of a restaurant and have photographers snapping pictures of Dad. The photographs would later run under headlines like, "Family Comes to Aid of Ailing Dean." Invariably, they would pick the shots that made him look the worst.

But it never bothered Dad. We'd lived with the paparazzi our entire lives, and that's just the way it was. In the good old days and the not-so-good old days, the press was always there. The media helped create the fame for Dad and my family, and he had a policy of taking the good with the bad. If Dad chose to go out, he knew how bad he looked and I know how hard that was for a man whose grooming had been immaculate. But he would never say, "How dare they take a picture of me looking like that." He knew the game. That was Dad. I'm going out to dinner with my family. Take your pictures.

Although his physical appearance worsened, it was only the last time that I had dinner with him that I noticed his mind was going too. Mom had called me at home in Utah, where Annie and I had just had our second daughter, Montana Sage, and she said, "Ricci, I think you should come see your Dad." The tone in her voice had me worried. We all knew Dad was in poor health—it was never one specific thing, just mostly problems you would attribute to old age.

I flew to Los Angeles and met Dad at the Hamburger Hamlet on a Sunday evening. We talked, and he mentioned to me he hadn't smoked for five years. I knew he had quit smoking, but only four months earlier. He was convinced, however, that he hadn't smoked in years.

Smoking was something that Dad had done almost every day since he was a teen. First, he puffed Lucky Strikes, no filter, and then switched to Kents. Cigarettes were always a part of Dad's ensemble, on stage and at home. While Frank cupped his smokes for a few puffs and rarely inhaled, Dad drew his cigarettes down to the butt.

In those early days, before the Surgeon General's warnings, secondhand smoke studies, and the tobacco lawsuits, everyone smoked. Dad smoked, Mom smoked, most of the adults smoked, inside the house, in the car, in bed, it made no difference. Cigarettes were a standard fixture around the house at 601, so ubiquitous that we kids took to placing them atop lampshades and in the fruit bowl.

On the fireplace ledge in the living room of 601, a decorative miniature replica of a knight's suit of armor stood guard for years. We regularly placed a cigarette in the mouth guard of the knight's helmet, and the maids regularly removed it. One day in the 1960s, a photographer took several photos of Dad for an upcoming album cover. Dad was sitting on the terrazzo ledge of the fireplace with his legs up, looking introspective. The photo looked great on the back of the album cover, especially if you were sharp enough to notice the cigarette sticking out from the miniature knight's mouth. I guess no one at Capitol Records ever spotted that little prank of ours in the photograph, because in 1998, when the record company compiled a compact disc of Dad's Christmas songs titled *Making Spirits Bright*, they ran the same photo of Dad next to the fireplace with our Sir Smoker next to him.

There's no doubt all of Dad's smoking contributed to his declining health, but it certainly wasn't the only cause. He no longer got his exercise with golf, and he was drinking more because he sat around more. But much of his ailment was a sadness that had grown steadily since Dean-Paul's death. It was compounded by the loss of other family and friends, getting older, the kids growing up and having their own lives, the divorces, and just the boredom he felt. In many ways, Dad had done it all and there wasn't much that interested him anymore. That sadness weighed down on Dad, and he did not have the desire or strength to push it away.

When I walked him out to his car at the Hamburger Hamlet that last evening together in October 1995, I felt that sadness around him. Just a few blocks up Doheny was our old neighborhood, 601 Mountain Drive. Our house was long gone, replaced by a modernistic concrete bunker that seems as inviting as a dentist's chair. We had such great times, so many memories. Now for Dad, those memories were sailing into the fog of forgetfulness.

We hugged. I told him I loved him. "Love you too, pallie," he said. "See ya later."

I called him periodically after that dinner, just checking on him. Because of our new baby, Montana Sage, Annie and I decided not to travel to Mom's house in Beverly Hills for the holidays that year. On the afternoon of Christmas Eve, I called Dad to relay our wishes for a Merry Christmas, but his cook, Connie, said he was sleeping.

A couple hours later I called his house, but there was no answer. That was odd, because while Dad rarely if ever answered his telephone, there was always someone at the house who would, either Connie, one of the guards, or the visiting nurses. I started to worry that something might be wrong.

Through the evening and into the night I called his home phone, which rang and rang. My feelings of anxiety grew, because I couldn't understand why no one was picking up. Annie and I stayed up well into the morning, putting together toys for the girls and wrapping presents. We went to bed at about 3 A.M., still wondering if Dad was all right and fighting the premonitions that clouded my mind.

About 6:30 A.M., the phone rang. It was Mort Viner, Dad's agent. "Ricci, your dad passed away last night," Mort said. "Your Mom is having me call the kids. Do you want to call Gina or should I?"

I told him I would tell her. Unlike delivering the news of Mom and Dad's divorce twenty-five years earlier, I didn't have any illusions that there was some silver lining to be found here. I called Gina and there wasn't much to say. I knew both of our hearts were broken.

Dad was 78 when he died early on Christmas morning in 1995. It had been early in the morning of Christmas in 1966 that his mother and my grandmother, Angela, had died at age 69.

No matter the official cause of any death—in Dad's case, the coroner called it "acute respiratory failure"—people die when their heart no longer beats. For Dad, his heart just wasn't in it anymore.

The funeral was in Westwood three days later, in the memorial park chapel that was first used for Marilyn Monroe's funeral. It was in the evening, not too late. Some of Dad's songs played in the background. Instead of his casket, there was a photograph of Dad and an Italian flag at the front of the chapel.

Rosemary Clooney sang "Everybody Loves Somebody Sometime" at the funeral, which seems like an inappropriate choice because that song has always conjured up an image of musical foreplay, two people meeting and falling in love, getting another chance at romance. But Rosemary's arrangement of the song and the way she sang it revealed a whole new dimension to the meaning of the words. It was mournful and touching, a tribute to a person that I was fortunate to have known and loved. Hearing her sing that song of Dad's, I had the same feeling I had during Dean-Paul's missing-man flyby. It hit me that Dad was really gone.

There were many of Dad's friends at the funeral, and Frank sent his regrets, preferring to grieve alone, which we understood. Everyone had kind, caring things to say. As much as we knew this had been coming, everyone in the family was numb. We all had lost a little piece of ourselves.

All of us went back to our lives and grieved in our own way. I cherished my life with him at 601 and later, those evenings at the restaurants, reminiscing. I replayed our last dinner together in my mind, thinking of his fuzzy mental state that night at the Hamlet. I replayed that scene again three years later when I learned that Dad had signed a new will just eleven days before his death.

During the early 1980s, Dad seemed to make a point of talking with each of us kids about how he was planning his estate. I was uncomfortable talking about it, as I'm sure my brothers and sisters were. Dad was wealthy, a millionaire many times over and, while it probably was prudent to discuss how he was preparing for this inevitability, just talking about divvying up the spoils of his life's work was difficult for me. He had provided so much for us growing up, not just monetarily, that I felt Dad didn't owe me anything. And I told him so.

"I always did this for you kids," he said, referring to his career. "This is what I want to do."

He had similar conversations with some of my brothers and sisters. Sasha later told me she remembers one day at dinner how satisfied he was that he had gotten the papers drawn up the way he wanted, which would liquidate his estate after his death and invest the proceeds in treasury bonds for gradual distribution to his children and former wives.

I never saw the will and never questioned the handling of Dad's estate after his death, a complicated process that took over a year. Then one day in the mail I received an accounting statement that reported the assets in Dad's estate. The first thing I noticed was that more than half of his money had gone to estate taxes, the so-called death tax. The estate had never been liquidated, and new executors had been named to manage his investments on behalf of the beneficiaries.

Confused, I obtained a copy of his will and saw that he had signed it less than two weeks before he died. The witnesses who were present when he signed the will were his housekeeper, an on-call nurse, and someone I had never heard of. One of Dad's guards, who had been with him for the last few years and cared deeply for him, later told Mom he had refused to witness the signing because he was uncomfortable with swearing that Dad was of sound mind at the time.

Many times in my mind I've wondered how shadowy and unsavory that moment must have been, with each character signing their name on the witness line. To this day, I don't know why a new will was brought into play so near Dad's death. How the new will changed from the old, none of us knows for sure, since we've never been able to find the original will that Dad spoke to us about. Whether Dad truly wanted a revised will or whether he understood he was signing a new will, I don't know. We will never know.

Regardless, he was generous to us all. The greatest gift he gave us was his love. The government has yet to find a way to tax memories. And those memories of Dad seem to keep earning interest. Four years after he died, I was in Los Angeles on business and found myself with time to spare before a meeting in Westwood. I decided to go to a movie at a cinema complex that happened to be next to the Westwood Memorial Park where Dad is buried.

I had not visited his grave since the funeral and hadn't planned to on this trip. I had needed some time to pass before I was ready to see such a physical reminder that Dad was gone. But on this day just after Christmas, I figured now was the time. I walked over to the memorial park and wandered for nearly an hour looking for Dad's crypt. I simply could not find it. Finally, I asked a gardener if he knew where Dean Martin was buried. He pointed me to a section of vaults and I followed his direction.

As I entered the section, I noticed a woman on a bench, reading a book, who scowled as if I was invading her space. I tried to look somber and began scanning the plaques on the marble walls of the mausoleums.

I finally saw Dad's small bronze marker, cast with his name, the dates of his birth and death, and four words that will always be synonymous with Dean Martin: Everybody Loves Somebody Sometime.

As I read it, I heard a voice calling my name. Not a voice in my head, but a voice behind me, saying, "Ricci? Ricci, is that you?"

I turned toward the woman on the bench, but she was glaring at two people approaching behind me, looking like a librarian who believes in capital punishment for whisperers.

I turned around and saw a woman and a teenager coming toward me, calling my name and laughing. For the life of me, I had no idea who they were or how they knew me.

"Ricci, it is you!" the woman said. "I can't believe it. I'm Meta Bishop."

Meta was from Pittsburgh, and I had spoken with her on the phone a few times since Dad's death, but we had never met. She was a member of the Dean Martin Committee in Steubenville, which puts on the celebration honoring Dad in his Ohio hometown. Meta was visiting California with her granddaughter Heidi for the holidays. She had made a side trip to see Dad's grave and had recognized me from family photographs.

We laughed at the coincidence and started talking about Dad and the family. Meta is a vivacious woman who has probably forgotten more about Dad's career than I know. I didn't realize how we were carrying on until I saw the librarian woman glowering at us, obviously angry that we had dared to chuckle in the graveyard.

Heidi took a picture of Meta with me in front of Dad's crypt, and we hugged goodbye. As they left, I shook my head with amusement. I had come to Dad's grave reluctantly, maybe to ask questions that don't have answers, ponder the imponderables. But the chance encounter with Meta reminded me of what Dad was really about. His mortal remains might be resting on this respectful if somewhat stuffy stage, but his spirit was out there with the people who appreciated his unassuming style and his sense of fun. In life and after, he seemed to be telling me, "Hey, pallie, don't take it all so seriously."

It wasn't only the famous who loved Dad, legends like Frank Sinatra, John Wayne, Montgomery Clift, and so many others. It was also the regular man and woman who cherished him. From the president of the United States to the shoeshine guy at the NBC studios, Dad was adored because he never put up a front, never tried to be someone he wasn't, and always remembered where he came from and who got him there.

I know there will always be those who interpret his nonchalant style as a sign that he didn't care about anything—his fans, his health, his family, his career. But it never adds up for me. His style didn't indicate a lack of sincerity. It indicated a lack of pretentiousness.

Dad once told me about finishing up filming one of his western movies on location in Mexico in the late 1960s. The shoot had taken a few weeks at a spot near a small village, and

Always remembering who got you there. Dad, 1964.

every day the people in the community had watched the movie being made.

The crew was striking the set and starting to pack up to leave. Dad had gone into his "honey wagon," the little trailer he used during the day, to change out of his cowboy gear into his regular clothes for the drive to the airport. When he came out of the trailer, the villagers were lined up on each side of the pathway to his car, standing shoulder to shoulder at attention. As Dad walked between them, they began whistling in harmony a song that one of the villagers told him was an old tradition to show honor to an individual who had earned the respect of the community. No one had seen anything like it before. Dad told me that walk to his car was one of the most moving experiences of his life.

As I headed back to my car from the visit to his crypt that day in late December, I whistled as I walked through the graveyard. And I thought: "Now that's livin', pallie."

Life in the spotlight until the end. Always leave them asking for more. Dad was 78 years old when he died on Christmas, 1995. (Allan Grant photo)